English Language Knowledge for Secondary Teachers

If teachers are to develop their students' English language skills successfully it is vital that they overcome any existing lack of confidence and training in grammar and language concepts. *English Language Knowledge for Secondary Teachers* is an accessible book aiming to equip secondary teachers with the knowledge they need to teach language effectively. It clearly explains the essential concepts for language study, introduces the terminology needed for 'talking about language' and shows how this knowledge can be applied to the skills of reading, writing, speaking and listening.

This new edition has been fully updated to take into account changes to the curriculum and developments in digital and new media language. Written by an experienced teacher and consultant, the book includes:

- all the grammar knowledge that a secondary teacher needs;
- contemporary language examples to which new teachers can relate;
- a companion website with numerous activities for use in the classroom linked to each chapter and supported by detailed commentaries to explain how these work in practice (www.routledge.com/cw/ross).

By making language teaching a fun and enjoyable experience, this text offers a refreshing resource for any secondary teacher daunted by the prospect of teaching grammar and language.

Alison Ross is an educational consultant, examiner and former English teacher and examiner.

English Language Knowledge for Secondary Teachers

Second Edition

Alison Ross

Routledge
Taylor & Francis Group

LONDON AND NEW YORK

Please visit the companion website at **www.routledge.com/cw/ross**

This edition published 2013
by Routledge
2 Park Square, Milton Park, Abingdon, Oxon OX14 4RN

Simultaneously published in the USA and Canada
by Routledge
711 Third Avenue, New York, NY 10017

Routledge is an imprint of the Taylor & Francis Group, an informa business

First edition published by David Fulton Publishers 2006

British Library Cataloguing in Publication Data
A catalogue record for this book is available from the British Library

Library of Congress Cataloging in Publication Data
Ross, Alison, 1949-
 English language knowledge for secondary teachers / Alison Ross. --
Second edition.
     p. cm.
Rev. ed. of: Language knowledge for secondary teachers.
1. English language--Grammar--Study and teaching (Secondary) I. Ross,
Alison, 1949- Language knowledge for secondary teachers. II. Title.
 LB1631.R636 2013
 428.0071'2--dc23
                         2012033452

ISBN: 978-0-415-63596-7 (hbk)
ISBN: 978-0-415-63597-4 (pbk)
ISBN: 978-0-203-08586-8 (ebk)

Typeset in Palatino
by Fish Books Ltd.

Contents

1

Introduction

The aim of this book is to provide secondary English teachers with the knowledge about language that they need and, perhaps, did not acquire during their own education. It covers the essential concepts for language study, introducing the terminology needed for 'talking about language' and shows how this knowledge can be applied to the skills of reading, writing, speaking and listening.

Using the website

There is a companion website for the book at www.routledge.com/cw/ross. For each concept or term introduced, there is an activity for teachers to use with students. The logo (@) indicates that there is an activity plus commentary. The abbreviations Y7+, Y12+, etc. suggest the year group for which the activity would be suitable. Of course, it may always be necessary to revise some concepts that were introduced in earlier years, hence the 'plus' sign.

The activities are numbered to match the chapter and the order in which they appear, so Activity 5.9 would be the ninth activity for Chapter 5. Most activities have a commentary, explaining the key teaching points. A link will take you from the activity to the commentary, and back to the activity if it would be useful to look at it again.

The book is divided into two main sections:

- **Section 1** – deals with grammar and the structure of language.
- **Section 2** – moves outside the scope of sentence structure to explore aspects of:
  - Phonology – the sounds of language and their effects;
  - Semantics – the ways words convey meanings via emotive and figurative language;
  - Discourse – the ways whole texts are organised;
  - Spoken language – some key differences in the organisation of speech; and
  - Electronic modes – the ways that new technologies have influenced language use.

The organisation of the book involved a common dilemma for teaching approaches:

'Where should I start?'

A 'top-down' approach emphasises the importance of the wider picture before studying smaller elements. It may be more effective to begin study of a Shakespeare play by watching a performance of the whole text. But perhaps important aspects of context need to be appreciated before this: the conventions of the dramatic genre, or the historical and social background. Close analysis of speeches and individual words comes later.

The decision to take a 'bottom-up' approach to language study in this book was not taken lightly. Although a focus on words and sentences runs the risk of being de-contextualised, there are some practical advantages in working up from the basic elements of language. The educational background of the readers of this book also influenced the decision. Many university degrees in English emphasise the study of literature rather than language. Although such courses involve the study of language in its wider aspects – genre, metaphor, rhetoric, and so on – finer details of grammar remain a source of uncertainty. This area is therefore tackled before the more familiar aspects.

The fact that the section on grammar is relatively long does not indicate that the *structure* of language is more important than other aspects of language in *use*, but rather that the grammatical terms and concepts are less familiar to readers under the age of fifty. The reasons for this 'gap' in knowledge are connected with the changes in educational policy over the last few decades. These are worth exploring.

Knowing about language or using language?

Debates about English education tend to focus on the relative merits of explicit grammar study versus exposure to a rich variety of language use. The most noticeable changes have been in attitudes to the role of grammar. Using an analogy, I would suggest that – trams are to transport policy what grammar is to educational policy. Both have moved in and out of favour in recent history. In the 1950s there was a system of trams or trolley buses in most cities. They were considered an efficient form of public transport. Then they seemed outdated and the whole system was dismantled. Around the turn of the century, the advantages of this mode of transport were recognised and tram systems were reintroduced. Some people complain about the expense and inconvenience. For others, trams have intrinsic value, but their role is important in the wider scheme of things: trams contribute to a more efficient and environmentally friendly transport system.

Changing attitudes to the role of grammar teaching have followed a similar path. From the eighteenth century until the 1960s, a formal approach to teaching the structures of language was accepted as the most effective way to teach English and foreign languages. By the 1970s, grammar study was seen as outdated and inefficient. These conclusions were based on research studies showing that explicit teaching of grammar had little impact on the wider skills of language use (Wilkinson, 1971). It was replaced by a 'language in use' approach, where the emphasis was on exposure to various forms of language, without the need for the terminology to describe language. Later studies cast doubt on the validity of these conclusions (Tomlinson, 1994). After decades of teaching English without any explicit reference to grammar, the National Curriculum (1989, revised in 2000) caused another change in the ways English was taught in schools. The reinstatement of grammar – as with trams – has been welcomed by many with nostalgia for bygone days, when rules were fixed and order prevailed. However, this is not simply a return to the grammar teaching of the past. The contemporary, 'streamlined' approach to grammar no longer emphasises the value of 'naming of parts' for its own sake; grammar is now seen to have an unfulfilled potential for its contribution to the wider scheme of things. As the linguist David Crystal comments:

> *The principle was evident: one should not teach structures without showing children how these structures are used in real-life situations; and, conversely, one should not introduce children to the language of real-life situations without giving them some means of talking about it precisely. Structure and use should be seen as two sides of the same coin – a view which is present in the guidelines which led to the new British National Curriculum course on English. But the question remained; how exactly can these two domains be brought together?*

> *(Crystal, 1998)*

The situation at the time of writing is not clearly defined. The National Curriculum and National Literacy Strategy no longer have the official status of guidelines, but the new National Curriculum is not due to emerge until later in 2012. A full programme of study for English (maths and science) will not be ready until September 2014.

However, it is likely that broad principles will remain. The concept of language variation shapes the overall statement of aims for attainment. Pupils should become aware not only of the conventions of Standard English but also of the ways in which language varies according to the different types of use by: reading a variety of texts, writing for a range of purposes, and adapting their speech for different contexts.

The requirements for Language Structure emphasise the importance of knowledge about the way language works. 'Pupils should be taught the principles of sentence grammar and whole-text cohesion and use this knowledge in their writing.' This knowledge about language can be applied to pupils' use of language, using a division into three levels of language structure: Word, Sentence and Text.

- At *word level*, there are applications to spelling and vocabulary.
- At *sentence level*, applications to sentence construction, punctuation, and awareness of Standard English in the context of language variation and change.
- At *text level*, applications to skills of reading, writing, speaking and listening.

The organisation of the book follows this distinction between levels of language:

Section 1

morphology	word level
word class	"
phrase	sentence level
clause	"
sentence	"

Section 2

phonology	word level
semantics	"
discourse	text level

The teaching approaches used in the book aim to combine knowledge about language with skills in using language. Before outlining these it is necessary to clarify the definition of 'grammar' – the subject of Section 1.

What is grammar?

When David Crystal was invited to provide a definition of grammar that could be understood by a bright child, he offered this: 'Grammar is the way we make sentences.' This is delightfully simple, but it is necessary to be aware of some differences in the way the term 'grammar' is used and understood. For a word that is mentioned so often in debates about education, its meaning is surprisingly elusive.

This is partly because of the emotive associations that the word has acquired. The title of 'grammar school' for those pupils who passed the 11-plus examination suggested that grammar was the preserve – and even the major concern – of the educational elite. Feelings about other school subjects, such as Maths, Science, History and Geography, are generally neutral. Knowing about grammar is often a source of pride, embarrassment or even resentment. For some people, the study of grammar is connected with order and discipline. The Conservative politician Norman Tebbit once suggested that there was a correlation between the loss of grammar and crime rates.

The distinction between prescriptive and descriptive approaches to grammar is worth noting. The first grammar books in the eighteenth century aimed to codify the rules of the English language. The approach was **prescriptive**, assuming that there exists one 'correct' or 'proper' way of structuring sentences. The model used by these writers was the Latin language and some of the rules they proposed are still accepted without question today. A frequently mentioned rule is that you should never split an infinitive. Fowler perceptively comments:

The English-speaking world may be divided into (1) those who neither know nor care what a split infinitive is; (2) those who do not know, but care very much; (3) those who know and condemn; (4) those who know and approve; (5) those who know and distinguish. Those who neither know nor care are the vast majority, and are a happy folk, to be envied by most of the minority classes.

(Fowler, 1965)

For those readers in group 2 – who do not know, but care very much – the infinitive is the base form of the verb, e.g. *to go*. A famous example of a split infinitive occurs in the introduction to *Star Trek*: 'to boldly go where no man has gone before'. The reason for saying that infinitives should not be split is based on Latin, where infinitives are single words (*vincere* – to conquer), so cannot be split. Many people challenge the assumption that what was true for Latin must also be true for English.

If a prescriptive approach functions rather like a guide to etiquette, a **descriptive** approach, as its name suggests, aims to describe the structures of language in more neutral terms. This involves awareness of language variation and change, in particular differences between speech and writing, formal and colloquial language, regional dialects and Standard English. Although a descriptive approach acknowledges that language may vary according to its context, Standard English is still 'prescribed' for public communication. The prescriptive approach, though diluted, is still apparent in attitudes to prestige of standard forms of language.

There is also some confusion between the terms '**syntax**' and '**grammar**'. Although the terms are sometimes used interchangeably to refer to the structure of language, some make a slight distinction. The official website for the Department for Education and Science uses 'grammar' as the overall term, distinguishing between 'syntax' and 'morphology'.

Grammar is the study of the way language is organised, especially the rules which are used between words (syntax) and within words (morphology).

(http://www.standards.dfes.gov.uk)

So, grammar – including syntax and morphology – may be defined as 'the way language is organised' or 'the way we make sentences'. In *A Dictionary of Stylistics* (Wales, 2001) grammar is explained as 'the study of form'. Others refer to the 'structure of words or sentences'. The metaphor of building, or construction, is common to all. But what sort of construction is a sentence?

What type of structure?

On the page, sentences may look like a linear, **two-dimensional** structure. However, it is misleading to regard language as individual words, linked one after another in a string. For example, if we want to find out what occurs before a verb and look at the order of individual words in these sentences, there is no apparent pattern:

Teenagers	*upset me.*	*teenagers*	*(noun)*
They	*upset me.*	*they*	*(pronoun)*

Their refusal to <u>move</u>	*upset me.*	*move*	*(verb)*
Swearing <u>loudly</u>	*upsets me.*	*loudly*	*(adverb)*
Leaving lights <u>on</u>	*upsets me.*	*on*	*(preposition)*

A more helpful analogy is a **three-dimensional** structure, such as one created from Lego building blocks. Although the smallest unit is a single brick – or word – larger forms, such as walls or roofs, can operate as elements in the structure. In language, these larger elements are phrases and clauses. The three-dimensional structure of language can be summarised as a hierarchy of levels:

TABLE 1.1 Levels of structure

One or more **morphemes**	combine to form	words.
One or more **words**	combine to form	phrases.
One or more **phrases**	combine to form	clauses.
One or more **clauses**	combine to form	sentences.
One or more **sentences**	combine to form	paragraphs and whole texts.

Section 1 moves up through these levels to sentence structure.

Another helpful analogy for the structure of language is the game Jenga, building a tower from wooden blocks. The object is to add, remove or replace pieces without destroying the overall structure. This is similar to the construction of sentences: a basic structure can be expanded by adding or substituting elements; more complex structures can be rearranged or simplified by removing elements. If essential elements are removed, the structure collapses.

In the simplest English structure, a single noun precedes a verb:

> *<u>Teenagers</u> upset me.*

But other elements can take the place of a noun. In the examples above, the basic structure remains intact in all the changes.

The noun can be replaced by a pronoun:

> *<u>They</u> upset me.*

Or by a noun phrase:

> *<u>Their refusal to move</u> upset me.*

Or by a noun clause:

> *<u>Leaving lights on</u> upsets me.*

The technical terms for these other elements all share the word 'noun', precisely because they have the same function in the structure (see Chapters 6, 7 and 8 on phrase and clause structure). Thus the basic structure of noun + verb remains constant. This analogy with construction games forms the basis for the teaching approach to grammar used in Section 1.

Approach to teaching grammar

Perhaps the most important aspect of the teaching approach is that it is based on language users' intuitive awareness of what is – or is not – grammatical. The activities in the book provide examples that can be used in the classroom. These activities invite the reader to use their implicit understanding of structure to develop confidence in the use of explicit terminology.

In conjunction with this is the use of authentic examples of language use, wherever possible. These are taken from a variety of sources, including literary and non-literary genres, contemporary and older texts. This provides breadth of study, encouraging pupils' exploration of a diversity of styles and showing the flexibility of language use in a variety of contexts.

Another important aspect of the approach used is that it is based on interaction with texts, in the belief that people learn best when they are actively engaged. Many activities are 'playful', for the reasons, and in the ways, described by Crystal in his book *Language Play* (1998: 187):

1. Children are used to playing with language, and encounter language play all around them.
2. Language play chiefly involves manipulating language structures.
3. A major aim is to improve children's ability with language structures. Therefore:
4. We should make use of their abilities in language play…

The type of 'play' used in the activities can be compared to construction games, such as Jenga, mentioned above. This active manipulation of structures is also based on the fundamental principles of grammar analysis. The academic terms used are: substitution, deletion, insertion, transposition. These are 'basic' in the sense that they are fundamental to the system of grammatical classification. Luckily, they are also basic, in the sense of simple to understand. The concepts can be explained in more concrete terms and provide tools for pupils to use in direct, active exploration of grammatical concepts.

The four tests

TABLE 1.2 The four tests

Substitution	See if you can take out one part of the structure and replace it with another. If so, the substituted part must have a similar function.
Deletion	See if you can remove some parts of the structure. This will show whether these are optional, or essential, elements.
Insertion	See if you can add extra parts to the structure. This will also show that these are optional elements.
Transposition	See whether you can move some parts to other positions in the structure. This will show which are the movable elements.

The use of these four principles leads to the final important aspect of the approach.

Form v. function

This approach to grammar emphasises the **function** of words, phrases and clauses, as pupils develop understanding of the ways that parts of the structure operate in relation to each other.

As each term is introduced in Section 1, confidence is developed by exploration of its function. This focus on role – or function – is a more reliable way of understanding concepts such as 'noun', 'verb', 'adverb', 'subordinate clause', which may have been introduced earlier, using definitions based on their meaning or form.

Grammatical explanations based on **meaning** are a familiar memory for most people.

- A noun is a naming word.
- A verb is a doing/action word.
- An adjective is a describing word.

Sadly, these quick definitions only help with the most obvious examples; authentic language use rarely provides clear-cut, textbook examples. For example:
Which are the 'doing words' in this sentence?

There was a deafening scream as the Twister began its plunging descent.

It would be reasonable to say that the words *'deafening, scream, Twister, plunging, descent'* are 'doing' words, as they suggest actions. However, the verbs are *'was, began'*, neither conveying much action.
Which are the 'describing words' in this sentence?

The drunk tottered into the alley, clutching a bottle of vodka under his raincoat.

There are no adjectives in this sentence, yet description is conveyed by nouns: 'drunk, alley, vodka, raincoat', or the verbs: 'tottered, clutching'.

Another approach is to define word classes by the **form** of words. For example, an adverb is a word that ends in *–ly*. This also works only for classic, textbook examples. This is because of the changing nature of the English language.

Unlike languages such as Latin, French, Spanish, modern English language no longer uses many inflections, ie. changing the form of words by adding suffixes. Pupils should be aware that the same 'letter-string' may function in different ways. For example, the form of the word '*light*' remains identical in the following sentences, but its role changes:

(See Chapter 5).

What word class is 'light'?

1. *This is a <u>light</u> suitcase.*
2. *I always travel <u>light</u>.*
3. *Have you got a <u>light</u>?*
4. *<u>Light</u> my fire.*

The approach in Section 1 explores the function of grammatical concepts by using the four tests outlined above. Their use is demonstrated briefly as a way of clarifying the role of word classes and consolidating the terminology.

Substitution shows that:

This is a <u>lovely/nice</u> suitcase.	*(functions as)*	*adjective*
I always travel <u>carefully/wisely/cheaply</u>.	*(functions as)*	*adverb*
Have you got <u>any money/my book/a car</u>?	*(functions as)*	*noun*
<u>Extinguish/enjoy/report</u> the fire.	*(functions as)*	*verb*

Deletion can be used to show if a word functions as an adjective or adverb, as these are usually optional extras. Nouns, verbs, prepositions, etc cannot be deleted. The following example shows which words can, and cannot, be deleted.

This is a (<u>light</u>) suitcase.	*adjective deleted*
I always travel (<u>light</u>).	*adverb deleted*
Have you got a <u>light</u>?	*noun cannot be deleted*
<u>Light</u> my fire.	*verb cannot be deleted*

NB. The word 'always' can also be deleted and therefore functions as an adjective or adverb. Substitution tests – *usually / rarely / often / never* – suggest it is an adverb, because of the *–ly* forms.

The other tests can be demonstrated in a further example:

My neighbours play music.

Insertion can be used as a test for adjectives and adverbs (see Chapter 5). One or more adjectives can be inserted before nouns.

	(*annoying young*)	(*vile modern*)
My	<u>neighbours</u> play	<u>music</u>.

Adverbs can be inserted in a variety of positions: before or after verbs, at the beginning or end of sentences:

| (*often*) | | (*loudly*) |
| The neighbours | play music. | |

Adverbs can also be inserted before adjectives, or other adverbs:

This is an extremely <u>light</u> suitcase.

The neighbours very <u>often</u> play music loudly.

Transposition is a useful test for adverbs, or adverbial phrases or clauses. Adverbs can often be moved to other positions in the structure.

I travel <u>light always</u>.

I travel light <u>when I go on holiday</u>.

<u>*Often*</u> *the neighbours loudly play music.*

<u>*At weekends*</u> *the neighbours play music loudly.*

Summary

The approach to grammar teaching and learning in this book can be summarised as follows:

- It is descriptive, rather than prescriptive.
- It explores a variety of authentic language use.
- It is based on intuitive understanding.
- Language structure is seen as three-dimensional.
- It emphasises the role (or function) of elements of structure with meaning and form as subsidiary.
- It uses 'playful' activities based on four tests.

A final word on the debate about English education: whether knowing about structure or using language is more effective. The writer Phillip Pullman characterises the essential activity for children as being 'playful' with language.

> *Fooling about, playing with it, pushing it this way and that, turning it sideways, painting it different colours, looking at it from the back, putting one thing on top of another, asking silly questions, mixing things up, making absurd comparisons, discovering unexpected similarities, making pretty patterns, and all the time saying 'Supposing...I wonder...What if...'*

> *(www.guardian.co.uk, January 2005)*

Yet the activities he describes are surely explorations into the structure of language. I believe that there is no need to choose either structure or use. Playing with – or using language – is not distinct from learning about language, but a means of doing so.

The layout of the book

- A glossary of key terms is provided at the beginning of each section. These are highlighted in bold in the margin when they first occur.
- The margin provides cross-references to other chapters and pages in the book.
- Boxes highlight intriguing examples at the beginning of each section of the text.
- Activities are numbered and are usually followed by a commentary found at www.routledge.com/cw/ross. Please note that some activities require no commentary.
- References provide the author's surname and date, with full details in the bibliography at the end of the book.

Grammar

2

The building blocks of language

The book begins with the smallest unit of grammar – the structure of words.

TABLE 2.1 Levels of structure

One or more **morphemes**	combine to form	words.
One or more **words**	combine to form	phrases.
One or more **phrases**	combine to form	clauses.
One or more **clauses**	combine to form	sentences.
One or more **sentences**	combine to form	paragraphs and whole texts.

Although it might seem that a word is the basic unit of language, many can be broken down into smaller elements. For example, the words 'smaller' and 'elements' both have a familiar word at the core, plus an ending that adds to the meaning.

small + -er

element + -s

The technical term for the smallest meaningful unit of language is a morpheme.

Everyone understands this at an intuitive level. Even infants show their understanding of morphology, when they create forms like 'goed' or 'foots'. We are able to use words without wondering where they came from or how they were formed. As the National Literacy Strategy comments: 'The uncertainty for teachers is how far to make this knowledge explicit' *(NLS: Review of Research and Other Related Evidence)* So, what are the benefits of providing pupils with terminology?

The study of morphology encourages pupils to notice words. Their knowledge of the structure and origins of English words can be applied to skills required in the English programme of study.

Pupils should be taught about how language varies, including:

- the importance of standard English as the language of public communication, nationally and often internationally;
- attitudes to language use;
- the development of English, including changes over time, borrowings from other languages, origins of words and the impact of electronic communication on written language.

The most obvious applications are at Word level for Spelling and Vocabulary: working out the meaning of unknown words.

Chapter 2 begins with the wider issues: attitudes to standard and non-standard English; varying degrees of formality in different situations. It then explores the principles of word formation and the origins of English words. Chapter 3 shows applications of this knowledge to reading skills and spelling.

Language variation

This section explores attitudes to words in the language, introducing the concepts of a standard language and language variation. The notion of Standard English is often seen as a straightforward issue for teaching: some forms of language are 'proper' and 'correct' and others are not. However, the existing Key Stage Strategy consistently links the terms 'standard English and language variation', acknowledging more complexity in language use. The choice of lower-case – rather than a capital letter – in their use of the term 'standard' English is significant as it suggests a more tentative attitude, rather than the notion of a fixed, absolute standard.

Non-standard forms, such as dialect and slang, are no longer regarded as 'incorrect' or 'ungrammatical'. However, this does not mean – as some debates in the media suggest – that 'anything' goes! Pupils must be able to use standard English in formal situations.

Glossary
slang   colloquial   standard English   non-standard   language variation / variety
language change   formality   formal   informal   situation / context / circumstances
genre   purpose   audience   topic   writer

Why are you dissing me?
Eminem complained that Nicole Kidman dissed him, but he disses his mother in songs.

What is slang?

How do you respond to the use of 'diss' in these quotations? Is this type of language **slang**? Not a proper word? Another sign of the sloppy way teenagers use language? Or of the dreadful influence of Americanisms?

In any language, the standard variety is regarded as having a special social status. Standard English, therefore, is the model for educated written usage. But language is not static. The linguist and writer Stephen Pinker commented in an online chat:

> As far as I know, all languages have slang. Indeed lots of standard words started out life as slang, such as 'mob', 'fun' and 'bully.' Even today, slang words such as 'to flame' and 'to diss' are coming into the mainstream. No doubt that happens in all languages, because words are not designed by committees, but have to be with a creative speaker who first coins the word.
>
> (www. wordsmith.org)

As Pinker points out, much language that is considered **standard English** now began as slang usage. Dictionaries record words that have come into the 'mainstream' of language use, and indicate whether a word is considered slang or **colloquial** (abbreviated to *colloq.*) rather than standard. Pupils should be aware of the date of the dictionary used, as the language changes each year.

Go to www.routledge.com/cw/ross for Activity 2.1, Using dictionaries to find out the origin and status of words. **Y7**

Attitudes to language variation

Activity 2.1 showed how attitudes to words change over time. When the abbreviation 'mob' was first used for a disorderly crowd, it would have been considered non-standard, but it is now a standard English word. It is frequently the younger generation that introduce new words

It is important – especially for teachers working with pupils in a diverse and changing world not to take a purist stance on **language variety** and **change**.

However, it is equally important to point out to pupils the effects of non-standard forms. Walter Raleigh (1926) makes this pertinent point:

> The strong vivid slang word cannot be counted on to do its work. It sets the hearer thinking, not on the subject of my speech, but on such irrelevant questions as the nature of my past education and the company I keep.

Go to www.routledge.com/cw/ross for Activity 2.2, The effects of non-standard language. **Y8+**

Varying degrees of formality

The concept of **formality** is essential for the understanding of language variation, but needs some clarification. In everyday language, the word 'formality' means roughly the same as 'formal', indicating the type of behaviour, clothes or language suitable for public, ceremonial occasions. In language study, the term has a precise definition: 'the ways language use varies according to the situation'.

Thus it refers to a range of language use, including **informal** styles, as well as **formal**.

Pupils should be aware of different **situations** for language use, and the way that language varies according to these factors:

- **genre** – the text type, including forms of spoken, as well as written language
- **purpose** – what is the writer/speaker trying to achieve?
- **audience** – who is the intended reader/listener?

Pupils are influenced by the language they encounter: predominantly spoken language and informal writing. Their use of such non-standard forms in other situations is often accidental and inappropriate. An activity such as the following asks pupils to notice how 'youth-speak' is deliberately used for a particular situation. The paradox is that the text is written by a highly educated professional; whereas young pupils are usually required to adopt educated, professional styles of writing.

 Go to www.routledge.com/cw/ross for Activity 2.3, Exploring the language of contemporary journalism. **Y8+**

Genre, purpose and audience

The use of non-standard forms can be effective if pupils are aware of the conventions associated with various situations. For example, the use of slang and colloquial forms is effective in **genres**, where a lively, personal voice is needed: talk with friends, dialogue in stories and drama, a first-person narrative.

The **purpose** of a piece of writing affects the degree of formality. Writing to inform usually requires a more formal tone, using standard English to ensure clarity of content. Writing to advise or persuade may benefit from a colloquial voice, but the tone needs to retain some authority, which might be lessened by the use of slang.

Consideration of the **audience** also influences formality. The use of slang can identify an in-group with shared interests. Although the use of standard English is the established convention for public communication, we can note some changes in attitudes. There is a trend towards increasing informality in some forms of public speaking and writing. The *Guardian* newspaper, for example, used the headline: *The boy done good!*

But the novice writer should be cautious about such innovation. Informality is restricted to certain **topics**: leisure pursuits, rather than serious news. The status of the **writer** is also a factor: where the credentials of the writer are well-established, the use of slang is accepted as a deliberate, rather than lack of skill. However, pupils are encouraged in their writing skills to 'use imaginative vocabulary'; 'exploit choice of language to achieve particular effects and appeal to the reader'; 'use language to gain attention'. The next section looks at the structure of words in more detail.

Word formation

This section introduces key terms that pupils need for the study of word formation. In order to understand the units that make up words, pupils need to distinguish between letters, phonemes, and morphemes.

NB A box ☐ indicates an element of word structure. An asterisk (*) denotes structures that are not acceptable in English. A question mark (?) indicates some doubt over whether it is an acceptable word.

Glossary
morphology   morpheme   letter   phoneme   syllable   word

What is a morpheme?

The Greek root of the word 'morphology' sounds daunting, but some people may remember the cartoon character Morph – a plasticine figure that could change its form. A similar idea is conveyed by words like 'metamorphosis', from the Greek word 'morphe', meaning form, and 'meta' meaning after or beyond. The new words 'morph' and 'morphing' are now in contemporary language to mean changing one thing smoothly into another. **N.B.** The similar word 'morphine', however, comes from Latin *Morpheus*, the god of sleep.

So, **morpheme** means a form, unit or shape, and **morphology** is the study of ways these units can be grouped together into a larger form. The idea of change is also relevant, as morphemes can be moved around (inserted, deleted and transposed) to change the structure and meanings of words. To clarify the precise definition of morpheme as both the smallest and a meaningful unit, we can relate it to more familiar terms and concepts: letters, sounds, syllables and words.

Letters, or **phonemes**, are contenders for the smallest unit of language, but they are not meaningful.

The letters 'p', 'i' and 'n' mean nothing in isolation.

Nor do the individual sounds – phonemes: /p/ /I/ /n/

Words may seem like the basic meaningful units: many words like *pin* cannot be divided further. But if you take a more complex word like *replaceable*, it is clear that it can be broken down into smaller parts.

Syllables are the familiar way of dividing a word into smaller parts – the beats that make up the rhythm of a word, often exploited in poetry. The word *replaceable* has four syllables:

> *re-place-a-ble*

But not all syllables convey meaning: *a* and *ble* .

Deletion test

The grammatical test of deletion can be used to show which units of structure are meaningful, i.e. morphemes. If we apply the test of deletion to the structure of the word 'replaceable', we see that some parts of the word can be removed, leaving a meaningful form:

> *replace* |*able*|
>
> |*re*| *placeable*
>
> |*re*| *place* |*able*|

This shows that the word is formed from three morphemes:

|*re*| |*place*| |*able*|

(meaning 'again')   (the core meaning)   (meaning 'ability')

We cannot delete any letter, or even, syllable:

> * *replaceabl* |*e*|
>
> * *replacea* |*ble*|

Thus a morpheme is *not* the same as a syllable. This distinction is tricky, as many morphemes are also a single syllable.

Types of morpheme

The terms **root** or **stem** both refer to the part of the word that conveys the core meaning and can stand alone. The term **suffix** is used for morphemes that cannot stand alone, but are added to the end of words; the term **prefix** is for morphemes added to the beginning of words.

Thus the structure of the word 'replaceable' can be analysed like this:

place	*stem/root*
re–	*prefix*
–able	*suffix*

N.B. Some textbooks use the terms 'free' and 'bound' morpheme for this distinction. The general term 'affix' refers to any bound morphemes. Apart from prefixes and suffixes, there are two other types of affix possible in word formation. As they are not commonly used in the formation of words in English, the terms are mentioned briefly:

circumfix	*an element added around the word structure*
infix	*an element added inside the word structure*

There are a few examples of infixes in non-standard contemporary English. These insert taboo words, e.g. 'abso-bloody-lutely'.

Go to www.routledge.com/cw/ross for Activity 2.4, which provides practice in identifying the structure of words. The pairs of words have similar syllables at the beginning or end. The deletion test shows whether these are morphemes – meaningful units. **Y7+**

Application to language variation

The concept of prefixes and suffixes can be used in exploration of language change and variation.

For example, the use of 'diss' (as in 'Don't diss me') shows a creative use of language, forming a free-standing new word from the prefix used in words such as:

dis–respect

dis–like

dis–agree

This may seem like flagrant breaking of the rules of English grammar, but is based on the principles of word formation. The same process has created these words:

hyper	*as in*	*hyperventilation*
mega	*as in*	*megawatt*
retro	*as in*	*retrograde*
pseud(o)	*as in*	*pseudopod*

Once only occurring as prefixes in scientific words, these are now used as free-standing words in colloquial usage. Attitudes to new word forms tend to change, as their use spreads into more 'respected' forms of language. The concepts of root, prefix and suffix will be used in the next section to explore the various patterns of words in English.

Identify lexical patterns

All words were 'new' at one time. This section emphasises the creative aspect of language use, and pupils' intuitive grasp of the principles by which meanings are conveyed. The key terms for types of word structure are introduced.

Glossary
neologism   word family   inflection   derivation   compound blending   abbreviation   acronym   onomatopoeia   clipping   back-formation

> *I've got a feeling of fullupness.*
>
> *Is a serious illness a killness?*
>
> *My beamish boy... He chortled in his joy.*
>
> *Roadrage and bluejacking on the increase.*

Creating words

Young children are excellent sources of **neologisms** (newly created words) as are poets and journalists. The new words are rarely created 'out of the blue', but formed from existing morphemes. In the first example above, a child joins three morphemes to create a new noun: 'fullupness'. The second blends the two words 'kill' and 'illness' to convey the idea of a fatal illness. In his poem 'The Jabberwocky', Lewis Carroll created many 'nonsense' words that are strangely meaningful: 'beamish' seems like an adjective formed from the stem 'beam'. One blend of the words 'chuckle' and 'snort' – 'chortle' – has passed into standard English. The new word 'roadrage' is now accepted, but many created words, such as 'bluejacking' (for the sending of offensive text messages) do not pass into standard usage.

N.B. Some linguists prefer to use the term 'lexeme' instead of word, to cover the range of forms that a single word may have: *walk, walks, walking, walked*. In this book, I will use the term 'word' for clarity and simplicity.

Word families

Language users can both create new words and understand unfamiliar words, by making connections with other related words. A group of words that share the same root, or stem, is called a **word family**. For example, the words 'magnificent', 'magnitude', 'magnate', *magnum opus* are all formed from the Latin root *magnus*. Even without a knowledge of Latin, it is possible to work out that all share the meaning of *large*. Other families of words share the same prefix (*repeat, return, redo*) or suffix (*readable, passable, doable*).

Pupils' intuitive understanding of morphology can be demonstrated in creative activities of word formation.

 Go to www.routledge.com/cw/ross for Activity 2.5, Creating new words from the root 'chew'. **Y7+**

Processes of word formation

Not only do users instinctively choose prefixes for the beginnings of words and suffixes for the endings, but they also order more than one affix according to the rules of English morphology. They understand implicitly that there is no scope for transposition – morphemes cannot be moved from one place to another in the structure of English words. For example, a complex word like 'un-re-chew-abil-ity' is felt to be 'grammatical', whereas the following are not:

> * *abil-chew-ity*
>
> * *re-un-chew-able*

Pupils should know the terms for different processes of word formation in the English language. This knowledge can be applied to grammar, as well as to reading and spelling. The addition of prefixes and suffixes to roots is the most common lexical pattern. Most words in English are formed by the process of inflection and derivation.

Inflection

This term refers to suffixes marking grammatical forms such as plurals and verb tenses.

> *–s marks the plural form of most nouns ('tables')*
>
> *–s also marks the third person of verbs ('jumps')*
>
> *–ing marks the progressive form of verbs ('jumping')*
>
> *–ed marks the past tense of verbs ('jumped')*

Modern English language has relatively few inflections in comparison with other languages. There is little scope for creativity in grammatical inflections, but some changes have occurred over time. In earlier periods, English used more inflections for verbs, e.g: *goeth* and *goest,* which have been lost in a process of simplification.

This has not happened in Romance languages derived almost exclusively from Latin. For example, the Italian verb meaning 'speak' has dozens of endings for person and tense:

> *parlo, parli, parle, parliamo, parlisti, parlaron, parlavo, parlando,* etc.

These languages have inflections for the gender of nouns. German also has inflections for the case (whether subject, object, etc.) of nouns.

In contrast, inflections that indicate case only occur in pronouns in English:

I, me, my, mine

English uses few inflections for nouns, apart from pluralisation. This is normally –*s* suffix, but the older form: –*en* remains in a few exceptions:

children, oxen

The suffix -*ess* is used on some nouns to indicate gender:

actress, waitress, manageress

The suffix –*ette* indicates diminutive size:

cigarette, laundrette, usherette

N.B. Gender suffixes tend to be avoided in contemporary language use, because they mark the masculine form as the norm, implying that the female version is subsidiary and – in the example of 'usherette' – actually smaller.

Suffixes –*er* and –*est* are added to adjectives, to indicate comparative and superlative:

big, bigger, biggest

Derivation

This process also uses the addition of prefixes and suffixes. Many existing affixes are used to form words with new meanings:

pre-shrunk

clean-able

anti-static

Some suffixes indicate a change in word class:

beam	*(verb)*	*beamish (adjective)*
happy	*(adjective)*	*happiness (noun)*
create	*(verb)*	*creation (noun)*

Proper nouns can also be used more widely, by the process of inflection and derivation:

hoovering	*– from the brand name Hoover*
sellotatape	*– from Sellotape*
thatcherite	*– from the person's name (Mrs Thatcher)*
macjob	*– from the company name (McDonald's)*

(See Chapter 4 on word classes and 8 on verb phrases).

N.B. Pupils' knowledge of inflection and derivation can be used to help identify word classes.

Compounding

This process is also very common, accounting for a high percentage of new words, formed by joining two words:

roadrage	*road + rage*
airport	*air + port*
coursework	*course + work*

> **(See section on spelling for further discussion of language change re the use of hyphens).**

Both compounding and inflection or derivation can be used to form words:

fullupness	*full + up + –ness*
or	
signposting	*sign + post + -ing*

In some cases, usually colloquial, three words are joined:

bad-for-you
in-your-face

Blending

This process is a type of compounding – both shortening and combining two words. It tends to occur in playful uses of language, with a few examples passing into mainstream usage:

chortle	*chuckle + snort*
killness	*kill + illness*
motel	*motor + hotel*
chunnel	*channel + tunnel*
slackademic	*slacker + academic*
rockabilly	*rock and roll + hillbilly*
bluejacking	*blue + jack + ing*

Abbreviation

This process is common, with the simpler abbreviation often passing into standard usage and the original form being lost:

fridge	*from refrigerator*
bus	*from omnibus*
pram	*from perambulator*

Some words are formed by a combination of abbreviation + derivation or compounding:

high-tech, celeb-wise, sitcom

N.B. The term **clipping** is used in some books for this type of shortening of words. The term **backformation** refers to a few words whose original form has been abbreviated, as if it contained a suffix. This process would not be noticed without knowledge of the history of the English language.

burgle	*a burglar (from Old French* burgier *– to pillage)*
letch/lech	*a letcher (from Old French* lechier *– to live in debauchery)*

Acronym

The use of initial letters of a phrase to form a word is very common in organisations. Only those of use to a wider group pass into the standard language.

GCSE	*General Certificate of General Education*
LASER	*Light Amplification by the Stimulated Emission of Radiation*
BANANA	*Build Absolutely Nothing Anywhere Near Anything*

Onomatopoeia

Some words are simply invented, the sound of the word resembling its meaning. In dictionaries, their origin is noted as 'imitative':

clatter

bling-bling

This explicit knowledge of terminology is not required before A-level language, but can be introduced earlier to encourage awareness of word structures.

 Go to www.routledge.com/cw/ross for Activity 2.6, Identifying the different processes of word formation. **Y10+**

Application to language change

This knowledge of processes of word formation can also be applied to language change.

The language of new technologies is a source of creative word formation. The language of the media also uses innovative word choice.

 Go to www.routledge.com/cw/ross for Activity 2.7, Exploring the use of compound words in magazines with a teenage audience. **Y10+**

The next section looks at the origins of English and shows how many words have come into the language by a process of borrowing from other languages.

The origins of English

In the words of the film *Life of Brian*,

Apart from the sanitation, medicine, education, wine, public order, irrigation, roads, the freshwater system and public health, what have the Romans ever done for us?!

The Roman invasion of Britain introduced not only the advantages mentioned above but also a large store of vocabulary. Many more Latin words came into the English language via French, in the 300 years of Norman rule after the Battle of Hastings in 1066. This period of language is termed 'Middle English'. Around this time, many words were also adopted from Greek, via Latin. Pupils should have some understanding of the origins of words in English; recognise links between words related by word families and roots; and work out the meanings of unknown words or use dictionaries.

Glossary:
etymology Latin [L]   **Greek [Gr]**   **French [Fr]**   **Middle English [ME]**   **Old Norse [ON]**   **Old English [OE]**   **borrowing**

> *The would-be ingangers from France were smitten hip and thigh and our tongue remained selfthrough and strong, unbecluttered and unbedizened with outlandish Latin-born words of French outshoot… The craft and insight of our Anglish tongue for the more cunning switchmeangroups, for unthingsome and overthingsome withtakings, gives a matchless tool to bards, deepthinkers and trypiecemen.*
>
> (Jennings, 1966)

Old English

The comic writer, Paul Jennings (*Punch*, 1966) provided the example above of what English might have been like if William the Conqueror had been defeated at the *clash* of Hastings. (The word *battle* has its origins in the Latin verb meaning 'to beat'.) A text avoiding any words of Latin, French or Greek origin sounds strange. Going back to the earliest roots of the English language, we find terms for basic concepts, but this does not make the text simple to understand.

Many of the basic words in English are of Anglo Saxon/Germanic (termed **Old English**) origin. These words are often monosyllables:

meat, wife, sun

But more complex concepts could be conveyed by combining words, as in the invented terms in Jennings' article:

overthingsome   *unbecluttered*

selfthrough   *unbedizened*

switchmeangroup   *inganger*

trypieceman   *unthingsome*

withtaking

The history of the English language can be traced further back to Celtic origins. However, very few Celtic words remain, mostly in place names or for geographical features.

pen   *meaning hill (as in Penrith)*

The Viking invasion introduced words from **Old Norse**. These are often also monosyllables:

get, give, hit, kick, law, take, they, want, window

Interestingly, many words of Norse origin can be recognised, as they begin with a 'sk' sound:

scatter, score, scowl, scrape, scrub, skill, skin, skirt, sky

In the early history of English, the language was affected by invasions from other cultures. In more recent centuries, the reverse has been more influential: travel, trade and colonisation all introduced new words into English. The increasing power of the English-speaking nations (including their media and technology) has affected other languages. As the Canadian journalist Mark Abley (2003) suggests:

> Modern English is the Wal-Mart of languages: convenient, huge, hard to avoid, superficially friendly, and devouring all rivals in its eagerness to expand.

The **etymology**, or origin, of words is given – even in concise dictionaries – in square brackets at the end of the definition. If abbreviations are used, these are listed at the beginning of the dictionary: **L–Latin; Gr–Greek**; OE- Old English; ON- Old Norse; **Fr–French**; etc. Although a detailed knowledge of the various origins of Modern English is not required before A-level Language study, pupils should be aware that the English they use today has borrowed words from other languages.

 Go to www.routledge.com/cw/ross for Activity 2.8, Exploring the etymology of familiar vocabulary. **Y8+**

The next chapter shows how pupils' understanding of morphology can be applied to the skills of reading and spelling.

3

Applications of morphology

This chapter shows how pupils' knowledge of morphology can be applied to word-level skills. The first section uses awareness of roots, prefixes and suffixes to develop understanding of unfamiliar vocabulary. The second section suggests some applications to spelling.

Applications to reading

Glossary
generative words   key words

> Paediatrician's house stoned by angry mob.
> Anti-natal classes?

Prefixes and suffixes

Efficient readers do not need to turn to a dictionary every time an unfamiliar word occurs. Apart from using guesswork from the context of the word, the ability to break down the word into meaningful parts helps to work out the meaning. This skill can be developed by understanding the meaning of prefixes and suffixes. In addition, the meaning of common roots from Latin and Greek is an aid. Of course, nothing in language is ever completely straightforward. Partial (mis)understanding leads to the unfortunate confusions between *paedophile* and *paediatrician* and between *ante-* (before) and *anti-* (against).

There are tens of thousands of words in the English language. These are formed from a smaller number of prefixes, suffixes and roots, but a full list would overwhelm any student of English. Paulo Freire's work on literacy in Brazil has been influential in many ways. The first principle is to begin with the vocabulary of the group or community. Freire (1973) believed that generative words should have special affective importance to learners and should evoke the social, cultural and political contexts in which learners use them. Then **generative words** are chosen to show how elements can be separated and recombined to form other words.

According to Freire (1970), in Portuguese, only fifteen words are needed to generate all the other words in the language.

In the English language, Brown (1971) suggests that there are 14 words that contain the 20 most useful prefixes and the 14 most important roots, which are to be found in over 14,000 words in a concise dictionary or close to 100,000 words in an unabridged dictionary size. However, his key words (such as *oversufficient*) are unlikely to engage the interest of school students.

Roots

I list some of Brown's roots below, adding some others of potential usefulness:

tend	*to stretch*
spec	*to look at*
fac	*to make*
duct	*to lead*
scrib	*to write*
mit	*to send*
pos	*to place*
cap	*to hold*
capit	*head*
corp	*body*
carn	*meat*
vert	*to turn*
ject	*to throw*
fort	*strong*
tract	*to drag*
noct	*night*
somn	*sleep*
pac	*peace*
mal	*bad*
ben	*good*

It is important to find a meaningful context for the study of key roots and prefixes. If we aim to engage pupils in dialogue and base learning in their own experience, teachers need to choose words that stimulate interest. Activity 3.1 draws on pupils' familiarity with brand names. These are usually invented words, which use awareness of existing roots to suggest the desired set of meanings.

 Go to www.routledge.com/cw/ross for Activity 3.1, Applying knowledge of roots to work out meanings. **Y7+**

Prefixes

Activity 3.1 showed how pupils can work out the meaning of unfamiliar words by understanding the meaning of key Latin roots. These are usually combined with prefixes. For example, the root *vert*, meaning 'to turn' occurs in a word family:

divert:	*turn aside*
revert:	*turn back*
convert:	*turn together*
invert:	*turn inwards*
pervert:	*turn strangely?*

Hodges (1982) claims that there are 14 key prefixes, which account for the majority (82%) of the 20,000 most used English words.

 Go to www.routledge.com/cw/ross for Activity 3.2, Using some key prefixes to form word families. **Y7+**

Application to language change

Although academics have listed the most commonly used prefixes, it is interesting to note how some rare technical terms have been adopted into colloquial language; not only the examples mentioned before – *mega, hyper, retro, hyper, pseudo* – but also:

anti-	
ante-	*('to up the ante')*
auto-	
contra-	
homo-	
micro-	
macro-	
mini-	
tele-	
trans-	*('tranny')*
ultra-	

It seems that more obscure words and morphemes are greeted with delight, rather than trepidation. In this spirit, teachers might extend the range further:

ambi-	on both sides, as in *ambidextrous, ambiguous*
proto-	first, as in *protocol, prototype*

Suffixes

Some suffixes are useful in working out the meaning of words. Many of these are intuitively understood:

-arium	a place, as in	*aquarium, solarium*
-ify	to make, as in	*liquify, codify*
-itis	diseases, as in	*bronchitis, colitis*
-ee	person affected by the action, as in	*employee, addressee*

The suffix -ism can indicate a state in a neutral sense: *baptism*, but new words tend to include a negative connotation: *ageism*.

-ism   action, state, now pejorative, as in alcoholism, racism

The suffix –wise is an interesting example of language change. Once only found in words of Old English origin:

-wise   way or manner, as in   *clockwise, lengthwise*

it is now used to form new words, usually with connotations of pop-psychology or business jargon, such as 'relationship-wise', 'profit-wise', 'viability-wise'.

Other suffixes are not so useful for decoding meaning, but will be useful in the study of the next level of language – word classes. They will also be used in some applications to spelling later in the chapter. These suffixes change a word from one class (type) to another. For example:

to nouns:	–age (from French)	*reportage, spoilage*
to verbs:	–ate (from Latin)	*aggravate, liquidate*
to adjectives:	–en (from Old English)	*leaden, wooden*

These are the only two suffixes that change words into adverbs:

–ly	*quickly, really*
–wise	*likewise, clockwise*

(See Chapter 6 for further exploration of grammatical suffixes).

One last suffix of interest for issues of 'correctness' and language change is the ending –um and –us on some nouns of Latin derivation. These suffixes were originally the singular form, with an inflection change in the plural:

(auto)bus	*? autobi*	now always	*buses*
syllabus	*? syllabi*	now commonly	*syllabuses*
corpus	*corpora*		*corpuses*
referendum	*referenda*		*referendums*
curriculum	*curricula*		*?curriculums*

The plural form of these nouns of Latin origin is now used for both singular and plural, with the original singular form dropping out of use:

medium   the media is/are

datum   the data is/are

Awareness of suffixes can also help with some common spelling problems, outlined in the next section.

Applications to spelling

Spelling is a source of pride to those who can and a source of embarrassment to those who can't. This section suggests strategies for pupils to address spelling difficulties.

Glossary
phonic   vowel   consonant   phoneme   homonym   hyphen

Why is English spelling a problem?

I'm raelly worierd abuot the delcine in good sllepping, and I'm not sure I even agere with the Cambirdge resaerch. I'd like to know mroe about the methodlogoy, the contorl grupps, the size of the smaple. And who kowns, it may just be anrother innernet joke. I've been saerchnig evreywerhe for the oriignal resaerch but I cna't fnid it. I even tried Goggle. Maybe I'm spelling Cambirge wrong.

This is the final paragraph of an 800-word article by Michael Johnson. Although nearly half the words are mis-spelt, it can be read and understood with little problem. As Johnson says:

Accroding to the exprets, the eye deosn't need or evn want the whoole wrord. It noets the frist and last lettres, and fills in the rest by inrefence. You can even add or dorp lettres. The jumumble in btweeen is irrveralent. Cogintion hapneps vrey fast and quite misteriollusly.

(*www.guardian.co.uk*, 2003)

However, the fact remains that spelling is assessed. It is a slight comfort to know of many successful people who are, or were, dyslexic: W.B. Yeats, Albert Einstein, Leonardo da Vinci, Winston Churchill, Richard Branson, Whoopi Goldberg, Eddie Izzard.

There is much controversy about the best way of teaching spelling: by exposure to the appearance of words, or by learning the sounds of letters that form words.

The **phonic** approach provides pupils with a strategy, but it is not always reliable. This is partly because the English language does not have a straightforward relationship between sounds and letters, but also because English is derived from various language origins.

There are 26 letters in the alphabet to represent 44 **phonemes** – meaningful sounds.

The 44 distinct sounds must be represented by various combinations of letters, rather than a simple one-to-one correlation, as in Italian, for example. Whereas Italian – and many other languages – derives from a single source, English has a number of different origins. The ways the letters are combined depends more on the language of origin than from any systematic rules. For example, the 'f' sound is spelt in different ways:

flaccid	*f*	Latin
gruff	*ff*	Dutch
enough	*gh*	Old English
photography	*ph*	Greek

Homonyms

It is not always the long, complex words that prove the most difficult to spell. Many short, common words are a problem, because they are so similar. The three related terms – **homonym, homograph, homophone** – all begin with the prefix *homo* meaning, 'same'. The overall term is homonym, which can be distinguished into two types of similarity:

Homograph – words with the same spelling, but a different meaning:

furniture polish / Polish people

a lead pencil / the dog's lead

Homophone – words with the same sound, but a different spelling and meaning:

read / reed

pair / pear

write / right / rite

Vowels

The discrepancy between sounds and letters is mainly in the vowels. There are five letters (+ *y*) for vowels, but English uses 20 different vowel sounds.

The following rhyme is used to alert EAL learners (of English as an Alternative Language) to the scope of the problem. It may also reassure native speakers who despair of ever getting to grips with spelling. If you read it aloud, you can see how words spelt in a similar way are pronounced differently.

(See Chapter 11 on phonology).

When the English tongue we speak
Why is <u>break</u> not rhymed with <u>weak</u>?
Won't you tell me why it's true
We say <u>sew</u>, but also <u>few</u>?
And the maker of a verse
Cannot rhyme his <u>horse</u> with <u>worse</u>?
<u>Beard</u> is not the same as <u>heard</u>,
<u>Cord</u> is different from <u>word</u>,
<u>Cow</u> is cow, but <u>low</u> is low,
<u>Shoe</u> is never rhymed with <u>foe</u>.
Think of <u>hose</u> and <u>dose</u> and <u>lose</u>,
And think of <u>goose</u> and yet of <u>choose</u>,
Think of <u>comb</u> and <u>tomb</u> and <u>bomb</u>,
<u>Doll</u> and <u>roll</u> and <u>home</u> and <u>some</u>.
And since <u>pay</u> is rhymed with <u>say</u>,
Why not <u>paid</u> with <u>said</u> I pray?
Think of <u>blood</u> and <u>food</u> and <u>good</u>;
<u>Mould</u> is not pronounced like <u>could</u>.
Why is it <u>done</u>, but <u>gone</u> and <u>lone</u>-
Is there any <u>reason</u> known?
To sum it up, it seems to me
That sounds and letters don't <u>agree</u>.

The most common phoneme (or sound) in English has its own name – **schwa** – as well as a symbol – This sound is made in the middle of the mouth and occurs in most unstressed syllables:

<u>a</u>part ('schwa' sound for the initial syllable)

This causes a problem for phonic approaches to spelling, as the schwa sound in unstressed syllables can be represented by various combinations of letters. For example:

a   comfort<u>a</u>ble

e   cin<u>e</u>ma

i   infin<u>i</u>te

io capt<u>io</u>n

This aspect of English phonology causes some common misspellings, by using the letter 'e' as the closest representation of the schwa sound in the unstressed syllable:

* *seperate*	not pronounced	*sep/ar/ate*
* *grammer*	not pronounced	*gramm/ar*
* *definate*	not pronounced	*de/fi/nite*

Spelling strategies

Because of these irregularities, a phonic approach to spelling can only deal with words spelt as they are pronounced. There have been moves in the past to introduce a phonetic system of spelling: ITA – Initial Teaching Alphabet.

George Bernard Shaw left money in his will to promote a regular system of English spelling. His famous example to show the illogicality of English spelling was:

Question: What does 'G-H-O-T-I' spell?

Answer: Fish!

The sound	*/f/*	spelled	*'gh' as in*	*enough*
The sound	*/i/*	spelled	*'o' as in*	*women*
The sound	*/sh/*	spelled	*'ti' as in*	*station*

But this attempt to simplify spelling went out of favour.

Many people find that they have a photographic sense of the appearance of the whole word and, while they cannot spell a word out letter by letter, they can tell whether it looks right. This leads to a word recognition approach, sometimes based on flash cards, but more often on providing as much exposure as possible to the written word in context.

See Chapter 15 on electronic media. Modern technology is affecting the use of standard spelling. This is partly because spellchecking programmes may be used as the source of correct spelling, rather than the individual's own knowledge. Obvious limitations of this tool are the problem of homonyms and the differences between American and British English spelling – the use of *–ize*, rather than *–ise*. The status of spelling is also affected, because the conventions of electronic communication (emails and chatrooms) do not emphasise the importance of correct spelling or punctuation – the priority is to convey the message as swiftly as possible.

The study of morphology can offer pupils some useful spelling strategies (rather than rules).

Deleting the prefix

Many common prefixes have a regular spelling. All prefixes have a single consonant, but are often misspelled as double. For example, Ambrose Bierce (2003) plays on the confusion between the prefix *mis-* and the word 'miss' in this definition:

Misfortune, n. The type of fortune that never misses

Deleting the prefix from the root can reveal some incorrect doubling of consonants:

*dissappoint	dis- **sappoint*	**diss-* appoint
* proffessional	pro- **ffessional*	**prof-* fessional

However, there are always complications. Why is there a double 'ff' combination in the word 'difference'? The reasons for this can be explained by looking at reasons for language change in pronunciation, which gradually affects spelling.

Consonant assimilation occurs to make some combinations of consonants easier to pronounce. The spelling of some prefixes has changed to reflect the easier pronunciation of some combinations of sounds. (This was probably a spelling mistake originally, but is now the standard spelling.) It would be tricky to pronounce the combination of sounds in the word:

*dis-ference

The easier pronunciation of 'dif-ference' is now seen in its modern spelling.

Other prefixes that have undergone consonant assimilation are:

ad–	to	*ac–*	*ac–commodation*
en–	to	*em–*	*em–power*
con–	to	*com–/col–*	*com–memorate/col–lective*
in–	to	*im–/ir–/il–*	*im–possible/ir–relevant/il–legitimate*

Deleting the suffix

The spelling of suffixes is more regular. Deleting the suffix provides a useful check for spelling.

–ful

This suffix is often confused with the related word 'full', causing such spelling mistakes as:

*success-full

*wonder-full

The suffix *–ly* is also mis-spelt. If the suffix is deleted, the correct spelling shows the word formation:

* beautifuly	** beautifu–ly*	*beauti–ful–ly*
* immediatley	** immediat–*ley*	*immediate–ly*

N.B. you can always be caught out, as this common example shows:

* truely	*true + ly*	*tru –ly*

Some words with the suffix ⨍able⨍ have altered the spelling to ⨍ible⨍. These changes are often – but not always!- after roots ending in 's' or 'se':

	–able	–		ible
teach	teachable	but	response	respons ⟨ible⟩
pass	passable	but	?	poss ⟨ible⟩
play	playable	but	reprehend	reprehens ⟨ible⟩

In the case of such irregular spellings, it is appropriate for pupils to use a spellchecker. For example, a common exception to the 'rule' offered above is:

use   useable   not * usible   or * usable

Unlike –able, other suffixes –age , –ity beginning in a vowel tend to drop the 'e' ending in roots. For example:

* useage becomes usage
* probeity becomes probity

The suffix ⨍–ent⨍ is often spelt -ant. For example, I am never sure how to spell words such as:

* independant   independent

This is because the unstressed syllable is pronounced with a schwa sound and could be represented by either 'a' or 'e'.

Changes in the pronunciation of English over time also involve vowel elision – the omission of vowel sounds. Some changes in pronunciation have passed into standard spellings. In these cases, it is the root of the word that undergoes assimilation:

* pronounce + –iation   pronunci ⟨ation⟩
* terror + –ible   terr ⟨ible⟩
* horrid + –ible   horr ⟨ible⟩

The omission of vowel sounds in spoken language causes some incorrect spellings:

* comftable   * comft –able   comfort – able
* buisness   * buis –ness   busi – ness

These common mis-spellings are less easy to explain by the rules of morphology:

* choclate   borrowed from South American language
* libry   ? libr –ary

Go to www.routledge.com/cw/ross for Activity 3.3, Using knowledge of morphology to clarify the correct v incorrect spellings of some commonly mis-spelt words. **Y7+**

I never know whether to use a hyphen or not.
Is it 'word processor' or 'word-processor' or 'wordprocessor'?

Use of hyphens

The use of hyphens is an aspect of spelling where an awareness of the processes of language change is useful. New words are often created to match a changing world.

For example, with the advent of steam locomotives, the tracks they ran on needed a name. Initially, the compound:

rail way

would be used as two separate words. As it comes into common use, such compounds tend to go through a process of hyphenisation:

rail-way

towards becoming a single word:

railway.

Thus the hyphen generally signals that the two words are approaching acceptance as a single word for a single concept. At this stage of the process of language change there is usually variation, with the two (or even all three) forms coexisting. Going to a dictionary for the definitive answer is rarely effective, as dictionaries are out-of-date as soon as they are published! Pupils should also be aware that a spell-checking tool on a computer is not the final word either.

 Go to www.routledge.com/cw/ross for Activity 3.4, Exploring variations in the spelling of some common compound words. **Y7+**

This brings the study of morphology to a close. The next three chapters deal with word classes. Although the most useful way of identifying types of words is by their *role* (the way they operate in language structure), pupils can use their knowledge of suffixes to recognise the *form* of nouns, verbs, adjectives and adverbs.

Words, words, words

This chapter moves from morphemes up to the next level of language structure: individual words.

TABLE 4.1 Levels of structure

One or more **morphemes**	combine to form	words.
One or more **words**	combine to form	phrases.
One or more **phrases**	combine to form	clauses.
One or more **clauses**	combine to form	sentences.
One or more **sentences**	combine to form	paragraphs and whole texts.

The ability to label types of words as nouns, verbs, and so on, is what many people think grammar IS. Perhaps this is because single words are the most obvious parts of language. But it is essential to recognise words as the first level of syntax. They form the basis for combinations into the succeeding levels of grammatical structure: phrases, which can then be combined into clauses, in turn forming the basis for various types of sentence structure.

However, the fact is that most of the terminology that people think of as 'grammar' refers to types of words, with relatively few for the higher levels of phrases, clauses and sentences. Many of these terms – noun, verb, adjective – have been introduced in primary school, but only with simple definitions that enable pupils to label simple text-book examples, but the question for teachers remains: Why is this explicit knowledge useful?

In the Framework, the aims of grammar study were to enable pupils to: 'understand and have the terminology to describe the role of word classes.' The emphasis is on *understanding* and the *roles* of different types of words. This may seem a minor point, but it is crucial to the study of word classes. The terminology is not used for 'naming' the words themselves, but the ways they *function* in language use.

There are three ways of explaining word classes:

■ a definition by **meaning** can only identify the most obvious examples;

- awareness of **form** (morphology) is a useful guide;
- understanding the **function** of each word class is the essential strategy.

The meaning and form of each word class is mentioned briefly, before exploring the function. Activities use the four principles of **substitution**, **deletion**, **insertion** and **transposition** to develop understanding of the ways words operate in the structure of English.

I hope other teachers will share the 'growing feeling that grammar teaching has an unfulfilled potential, particularly if it reflects contemporary English.' (NLS research ibid) Wherever possible, activities are based on authentic examples of language in use. The 'potential' of study of word classes is indicated in applications to:

- **language variation** – understanding the main differences between standard and non-standard uses of English
- **writing** – the use of appropriate style in more formal contexts
- **reading** – understanding the ways meanings may be implied by choice of vocabulary

This chapter begins by demonstrating the flexible roles of individual words in English and language users' innate understanding of grammar, before looking at each of the main word classes in detail. It begins with 'the nuts and bolts'- prepositions and conjunctions. Chapter 5 looks at nouns, determiners and pronouns. Chapter 6 looks at the remaining classes of verb, adjective and adverb.

Glossary
word class   **content v grammatical**   **open v closed**   **letter string**

A word, in a word, is complicated. (Pinker, 1994)

Language is a process of free creation; its laws and principles are fixed, but the manner in which the principles of generation are used is free and infinitely varied. Even the interpretation and use of words involves a process of free creation. (Noam Chomsky, 1970)

Word classes

The ability to name the different parts of speech – or type of word – is straightforward in a sense, as nearly all the words in English can be classified into eight **word classes**. Before exploring each one in detail, there is a useful, initial distinction: the word classes can be grouped as follows:

content/open classes	grammatical/closed classes
noun	pronoun
verb	preposition
adjective	determiner
adverb	conjunction

The first group contains the types of words that convey meaning in obvious ways, hence **content** word classes. In the second group, the words do not convey meanings in this obvious way, but function as the 'nuts and bolts' – or **grammatical** word classes.

A further distinction between the two groups is their size and capacity for change. There is a limited and stable number of pronouns or prepositions, but nouns or verbs run to tens of thousands, with new additions to the store, as well as losses. The terms **open** and **closed** refer to this aspect.

The terms for these word classes are mostly familiar, so why does Pinker say that a word is 'complicated' and why does the whole business of identifying nouns and verbs often cause so much anxiety? This is because words cannot be pinned down into a fixed class. A recognisable **letter string**, such as 'light', [see Introduction] can *function* as either a noun, verb, adjective or adverb. The potential of language for creativity and variation, as noted by Chomsky, is a double-edged sword: a flexible resource for users, but challenging for those looking for quick answers. However, the principles for creating new forms of language are not only 'fixed', but understood intuitively.

The next section demonstrates how pupils can use their intuitive understanding of the *roles* of word classes – the ways that they can *use* the same letter-string for different functions. The concepts of form and function will be used to explain each class of word. Activities draw on pupils' explicit knowledge of morphology – roots, prefixes and suffixes – to analyse the form of different word classes.

Glossary

verb   noun   adjective   form   function

A He <u>hitted</u> me. He's a puncher he is.
There I <u>unflatted</u> it.
I <u>hammed</u> those all by myself.

B I'm <u>souping</u>.
I'm <u>darking</u> the sky.
<u>Put</u> me that broom.
Let's get <u>brooming</u>.

C I'm <u>swimming</u> my duck.
These flowers are <u>sneezing</u> me.
I can't <u>die</u> this spider.
I'm going to <u>fall</u> this on her.

D How do you <u>sharp</u> this?
<u>Full</u> this up.
You have to <u>scale</u> it.
I'm going to <u>earth</u> this.
Why didn't you <u>jam</u> my bread?

> *E*   *I <u>hate</u> you and I'll never <u>unhate</u> you or nothing.*
> *How did you <u>unsqueezed</u> it?*

'Virtuous errors'

These are examples of the language use of children aged 3-4 years. (Peccei, 1994) Young children use their limited repertoire of words in creative ways to express themselves. Chomsky uses the term 'virtuous errors' for examples of child language that depart from standard, adult language, but demonstrate an intuitive grasp of underlying rules of grammar. A parrot, or a computer, can *imitate* words, but children effortlessly *create* new, meaningful forms of language.

The clearest examples of a child's intuitive grammar occur in their creative use of **verbs.** Although the root may not be a conventional verb, they use standard verb **forms** to express a variety of **functions**.

The explicit study of child language acquisition is part of A-level language study.

 Go to www.routledge.com/cw/ross for Activity 4.1, for Ways of exploring *how* a child creates new forms of language. **Y12+**

Changing the role of words

This creative ability goes 'underground' while children learn standard forms of language. It re-emerges in the innovative language of literature and advertising.

'He unseam'd him from the nave to the chaps.'	*(Macbeth, Act 1, Scene 2)*
'You've been Tangoed!'	*(Advert for soft drink)*

In both these examples we see words that were originally nouns – 'seam' and 'Tango' – used as verbs. Pupils can demonstrate this ability to change word class in activities such as the following. This shows that many words, or 'letter-strings', can be used for various functions. Words normally used as nouns can change their form to function as verbs.

 Go to www.routledge.com/cw/ross for Activity 4.2, with Ideas for creating verbs from nouns. **Y9+**

Application to language variation and change

This process of changing nouns to verbs occurs in language change, with many examples now accepted as standard English: *'chair* a meeting'. In contemporary language use, this type of change to word class is often associated with business jargon, or Americanisms, and thus disliked:

Can you <u>action</u> this?
Let's <u>flag</u> it up.

Similar activities can explore other types of words that can be used as verbs:

adjective: *big*   verb: <u>*Big*</u> *me up!*
preposition: *up*   verb: *She <u>upped</u> and left.*

There is no accepted term for these changes in the role of words, but the term 'nominalisation' refers to changes from verb to noun. Before looking at the content word classes – noun, verb, adjective and adverb – the following sections deal with two grammatical word classes: prepositions and conjunctions.

Grammatical word classes

Think of words as instruments characterized by their use, and then think of the use of a hammer, the use of a chisel, the use of a square, of a glue pot, and of the glue.

(Wittgenstein, The Blue Book, *1965*)

The study of word classes often begins with nouns, verbs, adjectives and adverbs, as the content words have the more obvious uses of 'hammers and chisels'. In order to understand their roles, however, it is helpful to recognise the 'glue' in the structure of English. These are the grammatical word classes, used in full sentences, but omitted in abbreviated forms, such as notices and headlines. The days of sending telegrams are gone, but such condensed messages illustrate language with only content words. Pupils will intuitively fill in the gaps with grammatical words to make the meaning precise.

 Go to www.routledge.com/cw/ross for Activity 4.3, Showing the function of grammatical word classes.

The final sections in this chapter deal with two grammatical word classes - conjunctions and prepositions.

Conjunctions

connective   **conjunction**   **co-ordinating**   **conjunction**   **subordinating**   **conjunction**

Some of the grammatical words added in the previous activity function as links. The term **connective** is used as an overall term for a variety of ways of linking structures:

Conjunction	*The clothes were too expensive, so they only bought a pair of jeans.*
Adverb	*They bought a pair of jeans, before returning home.*
Non-finite verb	*Disappointed by the trip, they returned home.*

This section provides a brief introduction to the word class of conjunctions.

(See Chapter 10 for further exploration of sentence structure).

Types of conjunction

The term **conjunction** indicates the function of this word class – to join parts of the structure together. The most frequently used conjunction is the word 'and'. It is used to express a simple sequence of items or events. It also the first tool that children acquire for creating longer stretches of language. For these reasons, the use of 'and' has an impact on style.

Co-ordinating conjunctions

The distinction between co-ordinating and subordinating conjunctions helps to explain some stylistic differences. There are only four **co-ordinating** conjunctions:

and, but, so, or.

Their function is to link parts in a straightforward way: expressing addition, opposition, consequences or alternatives. The resulting structure can be compared to a linear string of links. The television comedy *Little Britain* creates the voice of an inarticulate teenager, Vicky Pollard, by the repeated use of these simple conjunctions:

'Yeah, but no, but so, anyway…'

 Go to www.routledge.com/cw/ross for Activity 4.4, Identifying the use and effect of conjunctions in a literary text. **Y10+**

Application to style and formality

Pupils should be able to recognise repeated use of co-ordinating conjunctions as a marker of a simple – even childlike – style. One aim for their own writing skills, however, is to develop a repertoire of conjunctions to form a variety of sentence structures. The repeated use of *and*, *but* and *so* is often an indication of a lower level of achievement.

(See Chapter 10 on compound sentences).

Subordinating conjunctions

Subordinating conjunctions combine structures in a more complex way. This can be compared to a three-dimensional model, with structures 'embedded' within the sentence.

Unless dinner money is paid on Monday, pupils will not be able to have a school meal, as they must be ordered in advance.

This word class is closed, so it is possible to list all conjunctions. Some common subordinating conjunctions are:

because, as, since, so, although, unless, if, when, which, while

(See Chapter 10 on sentence structure).	These conjunctions express various relationships with the main clause: reasons, consequences, examples, exceptions, etc.

A rule often quoted is 'You should never start a sentence with a conjunction.' This, like most rules, is over-simple. It only refers to the three co-ordinating conjunctions, 'and', 'but', 'or'. Sentences can – and often do – begin with subordinating conjunctions: 'although', 'unless', etc. And yet there are many examples of sentences beginning with 'and'! Departing from this norm emphasises it a stylistic device. Pupils should be aware that the normal role of co-ordinating conjunctions to link parts of structure. These stylistic issues are discussed further in Chapter 10 on sentence structure and in Chapter 13 on Discourse.

Conjunctions summary

TABLE 4.2 Conjunctions summary

Function	Co-ordinating conjunctions normally occur as links between parts of the sentence. Subordinating conjunctions occur at the beginning of a clause and can be placed at the beginning of a sentence.
Form	Conjunctions do not change their form.
Meaning	Conjunctions express various relationships between parts of the sentence: addition, opposition, cause, effect, etc.

Prepositions

The examples below show a few differences between standard and non-standard uses of prepositions. Native speakers of English, however, intuitively use prepositions accurately. In addition, prepositions are a closed word class, with a finite number of members, so this section will be relatively brief. The ability to recognise prepositions will be used in Chapter 7 in the study of noun and adverbial phrases.

Glossary
preposition   phrasal verb

> *Get off of it.*
>
> *You shouldn't of done it.*
>
> *This is something I will not put up with.*
>
> *Ending a sentence with a preposition is something up with which I will not put.*
>
> *I parked the van in back of the house.*
>
> *I can't come out while ten o'clock.*

Prepositions with nouns

The term **preposition** itself indicates the function of this word class: their position is commonly before (*pre-*) nouns. They can convey meanings such as *position* in time and space.

Substitution test

 Go to www.routledge.com/cw/ross for Activity 4.5, Using the substitution test to increase pupil's knowledge of prepositions. **Y7+**

Prepositions with verbs

Although prepositions often occur before nouns, they can also function after verbs. This use is common in English, creating a variety of **phrasal verbs** with complex shades of meaning. These are tricky for learners of English, but are used effortlessly by native speakers. Their use tends to be informal, as there is often a more formal alternative. For example:

> *I can't* <u>*put up with*</u> *noise.*
>
> *I can't* <u>*tolerate*</u> *noise.*

 Go to www.routledge.com/cw/ross for Activity 4.6, Exploring some common phrasal verbs. **Y9+**

Applications to standard English

Prepositions are generally used without problem, but there is sometimes confusion in the use of 'of' and 'off'. The examples at the beginning of the section showed some common errors.

'Get off of it.'

The colloquial use of both prepositions is considered non-standard, so should be avoided in formal situations.

'You shouldn't of done it.'

A much stronger warning is needed in errors such as this. It is becoming so common that its use was noted in a letter from Central Trains:

> *You should of complained to the official present on the train.*

This type of error is influenced by spoken language, where the abbreviated form of *have* may sound like *of*. However, its use in written language is highly stigmatised, as it is clearly ungrammatical. A substitution test demonstrates that prepositions cannot function in this role.

> *should*   *<u>of</u>*   *come.*
>   ** on*
>   ** in*
>   ** with*

'This is something I will not put up with.'

The third example is less clear-cut. Prescriptive grammars used to prohibit the use of prepositions at the end of sentences. This view is mocked in the 'correct' version:

> *Ending a sentence with a preposition is something up with which I will not put.*

In contemporary use, prepositions often occur at the end of sentences:

> *I need more money to live <u>on</u>.*
> *I got the job I applied <u>for.</u>*
> *Who did you go <u>out with</u>?*
> *Noise is something I can't put <u>up with</u>.*

The effort to avoid this leads to rather clumsy, hyper-formal constructions:

> *I need more money on which to live.*
> *I got the job for which I applied.*
> *Out with whom did you go?*
> *Noise is something up with which I cannot put.*

This is one example of changing attitudes to grammar – if a structure is effective in conveying meaning, then it is acceptable in use.

'I parked the van in back of the house.'

There is some variation between standard US English and standard British English. US English can use 'in back of' as the opposite of 'in front of', showing the tendency for US English to retain regular patterns – as in the example of the verb 'gotten' vs 'got'. See Chapter 6, page 69.

'I can't come out while ten o'clock.'

In some northern dialects of English, the preposition 'while' is used in place of 'until'. This can cause ambiguity:

> *Vehicles must wait until the barrier is raised.*
>
> *Vehicles must wait while the barrier is raised.*

Preposition Summary

TABLE 4.3 Prepositions summary

Function	occur before nouns, after verbs, or *alone as adverbs*
Form	simple morphemes, with no addition of suffixes
Meaning	position in time or space, possession, accompaniment, etc. In phrasal verbs, they convey a variety of meanings

The two remaining grammatical word classes – determiners and pronouns – are explored in the next chapter, as they always function with nouns.

Nouns and pronouns

Nouns have a significant role in any language. There are hundreds of thousands of words in English and the majority of these are nouns. The first words a child speaks are mainly nouns for the important people and things in their world. Attempts to communicate with chimpanzees use pictures to represent objects. Perhaps the origins of language began with nouns? The need to identify new phenomena accounts for a large part of language change: most of the entries in any Dictionary of New Words are nouns, with fewer additions to verbs and adjectives.

Clearly the need to name our world of experience is a vital function of language. But the simple definition – 'a noun is a naming word' – is not a reliable way of identifying all nouns. It works for obvious, textbook examples – 'house', 'dog', 'tree' – where there is immediate agreement. As soon as there is doubt over more tricky examples, the debate has nowhere to go. If you ask pupils to identify the 'naming words' in this paragraph, they might reasonably pick out 'name', 'language', 'word', 'textbook', 'agreement'. Some of these words are nouns, but 'name' is definitely not, and 'textbook' is debatable. Other nouns may be overlooked: 'way', 'world', 'function'. How can teachers explain that 'name' is not a naming word; that 'textbook' may be the name of something, but is used in a different way here; that 'function' is a noun, even if it doesn't seem to name anything?

The approach to grammar throughout the book is to concentrate on the *structure* of language. Words operate in this structure in different ways. The term 'noun' is not so much a label for a type of word, but for the *role* – or *function* – it plays in a particular sentence. The four key principles of substitution, insertion, deletion and transposition can demonstrate the function of any word class in a clear, straightforward way.

Activities use these tests to develop pupils' understanding of the role of nouns and the related grammatical classes: determiner and pronoun. The examples used of authentic language are often creative and unusual, defying quick answers. But this teaching approach is based on the belief that the best way to explore grammar is by asking questions. Equipped with these skills, teachers and pupils can resolve any doubts in a systematic way.

The ability to identify different types of noun – common v. proper; mass v. count; concrete v. abstract – is rarely explicitly tested, but it has useful applications. It can explain some differences between standard and non-standard forms of English, as well as levels of formality and implied meanings. The first section begins with the 'nuts and bolts' of English structure – determiners.

Glossary			
determiner	article	demonstrative	possessive

> *Train delay funeral anguish.*
> *Climbers trapped on mountain.*
> *Entry without permit forbidden.*
> *Put cup on table.*

Determiners

Some 'little' grammatical words are used all the time, but hardly noticed. Because they do not convey meaning in an obvious way, they can be omitted, leaving the nouns and verbs to carry the message.

 Go to www.routledge.com/cw/ross for Activity 5.1, Using such abbreviated forms of language to draw attention to this 'invisible' word class. **Y7+**

What is a determiner?

The words highlighted in the previous activity are determiners. The immediate problem with the term **determiner** for this word class is its unfamiliarity. It may seem an unnecessary complication to introduce new terminology, when **article** is already familiar as a label for the two common words 'a' and 'the'. But many other words can operate in this role. It is useful to have one overall term to describe this word class, before learning the labels for each individual word: 'possessive pronoun', 'demonstrative article', etc.

Determiners can be explained by their *meaning*: they express concepts such as number and quantity. The *form* of determiners is relatively constant: they rarely change, by the addition of suffixes or prefixes. The most useful definition is the way they *function*: determiners are words that come before nouns. The function can be explored by using the key tests.

Substitution test

The substitution test can be used to show which other words share the same role as the familiar determiners *a* and *the*.

 Go to www.routledge.com/cw/ross for Activity 5.2, Exploring the range of words that can function as determiners. **Y7+**

Applications to style and levels of formality

There are specific terms for three sub-classes of determiner: article, demonstrative and possessive. These terms can be used to explain some common differences between standard and non-standard – or dialectal – uses of English.

The use of the **definite article** – *the* – accounts for one difference: in some dialects of spoken English, it is omitted or abbreviated:

> *Put (t) cup on (t) table.*

The term **demonstrative** includes the words: 'this', 'that', 'these', 'those'. This term can highlight a non-standard use of determiner:

> *Give me * <u>them</u> books.*
>
> *Give me <u>those</u> books.*

Possessive, as the name suggests, refers to words such as: 'my', 'your', 'her', 'his', 'its'. These can be replaced by any name, such as 'Alison's', 'Fred's', etc. This causes a common mistake in the use of the apostrophe. Although expressing 'possession', the determiners have no apostrophe. This is clearly not possible for most – *hi's* – but the distinction between 'its' and 'it's' is often confused.

> *The dog was chasing *it's tail.*
>
> *The dog was chasing its tail.*

NB. Words such as 'my', 'our', 'his', 'her' may seem to have more in common with 'pronouns', as they are related to words such as 'I', 'we', 'he', 'she'. They belong to the word class of determiner, however, because they perform the same role in sentence structures. A later section explores the different role of pronouns.

Insertion and deletion tests

The examples so far have shown a straightforward use of determiners – occurring immediately before a noun. But often the structure is more complex, including other types of words before a noun. The tests of insertion and deletion can be used to distinguish determiners from adjectives and nouns.

Other types of words can be inserted before nouns to provide additional information.

> *Put some <u>coffee</u> cups on those <u>side</u> tables.*
>
> *The <u>high-speed</u> train hit a <u>parked</u> car.*

Determiners are generally essential to the grammatical structure – they cannot be deleted in most written texts. Other types of words can be deleted, as the following activity shows.

 Go to www.routledge.com/cw/ross for Activity 5.3, Using the deletion test to confirm the role of determiners. **Y10+**

Determiners in summary

TABLE 5.1 Determiners summary

Function	always occur before nouns – cannot be deleted
Form	often single morphemes with no addition of suffixes or prefixes
Meaning	can express meanings such as number or quantity

The next section moves from determiners to nouns, as the two classes operate together in English structures.

Identifying types of nouns

This section uses pupils' intuitive awareness of language use to develop an explicit understanding of the terms for different types of nouns. It also introduces the concept of 'nominalisation'. This knowledge can be applied to understanding of degrees of formality and the ways meanings are implied in texts.

Glossary
noun   proper v common noun   abstract v concrete noun
mass v count noun   nominalisation

What is a noun?

> *What is a must?*
> *Stop being such a know-it-all.*
> *The unbearable lightness of being.*

The most familiar definition is based on the *meaning* this class of word conveys:

> *a noun is a naming word.*

This is not the most useful or reliable way of understanding what a noun is. Thinking about meaning may not help pupils to identify 'must', 'know-it-all' or 'being' as nouns in the examples above. (The first example was a question referring to a poster: 'Windsor Castle is a Must'. The third is the title of a book.) However, the notion of naming words can be used in a preliminary activity to collect some examples of 'classic' nouns. Pupils may have been told what some of their first words were. These are often nouns, used to name – or ask for – important people and things in their world, such as:

> *mummy, daddy, baby, ball, dog, cat, juice, milk, biscuit, shoe, car*

Even with such apparently straightforward examples of nouns, some caution is needed. As Chapter 4 showed, it is not possible to identify the class of a word in isolation. Many words normally encountered as nouns can be used in different ways. In order to identify the class, the word must be seen in context. For example, the word *baby* may be used as a verb:

> *Don't baby me.*

Thus, the fundamental definition of any word class is based on its *function*. Words are classified as nouns because they operate in similar ways in the structure of language. The four tests of substitution, insertion, deletion and transposition show how nouns are used in English structure.

Substitution test

Pupils can use their store of known nouns in substitution tests to see whether an unfamiliar word is a noun. If you can replace a word with a noun, that suggests that those words share the role of noun. The structure should remain grammatical, even though the sense might be strange. For example:

I want more <u>ticky</u>.	*Give the <u>wug</u> to me.*	*We need your <u>compliance</u>.*
juice	*ball*	*car*
milk	*mummy*	*biscuit*

Go to www.routledge.com/cw/ross for Activity 5.4, Using the substitution test to identify unusual nouns. **Y7+**

Form

Another way of identifying nouns is based on their *form*. Nouns can change their form to indicate singular or plural. Another change in form indicates possession. Pupils can use their knowledge of morphology to identify the types of suffix that can be added to nouns. Awareness of the close connection between determiners and nouns can be consolidated in such activities.

Go to www.routledge.com/cw/ross for Activity 5.5, Exploring the form of nouns. **Y7+**

Insertion and deletion tests

This knowledge of form can be used to identify nouns, by using the tests of insertion or deletion.

 Go to www.routledge.com/cw/ross for Activity 5.6, Using knowledge of suffixes to identify unusual nouns. **Y10+**

These aspects of form and function can be used to explain sub-classes of noun:

common	*vs*	*proper*
concrete	*vs*	*abstract*
countable	*vs*	*mass*

Common v. proper nouns

One important distinction is between **common** and **proper nouns**. This knowledge can be applied to the use of capital letters and to explore aspects of language variation and change.

Literature or literature?

One God or many gods?

The internet or the Internet?

Save now with abbey.

e e cummings

We've got a lot of Hayleys in Year 9.

Proper nouns are often defined by their *meaning*: names of people, places and organisations. They are distinguished in writing by the use of a capital letter, but the examples above show some variation. The same letter-string can be used as a proper or common noun: *literature* and *Literature*.

 Go to www.routledge.com/cw/ross for Activity 5.7, Using the insertion test to explore some differences in the *form* and *function* of **proper** v **common nouns. Y7+**

Applications to language variation and change

The meaning, form and function of proper v. common nouns can be used to explain the distinction between:

Literature	*literature*
God	*god*

Internet	*internet*
Abbey	*abbey*
E. E. Cummings	*e e cummings*
Hayley	*Hayleys*

Capital letters are used in English to confer a sense of respect and uniqueness, when referring to God or literature. The lower case suggests a more general reference. The poet, e e cummings, did not use this distinction in his poetry, nor for his own name. This trend can be seen in contemporary brand names, perhaps appearing more modern and unassuming. It is also common in language use in emails and text-messages, where capital letters are often omitted for names or the personal pronoun 'I'. It is important for pupils to use the appropriate style, when writing in more formal situations.

Even when names of individual people or organisations are represented with a lower-case initial letter, they still function like proper nouns – they do not take a plural form or follow a determiner.

*I'm banking with the barclay.

When names are used as common nouns – taking a determiner or a plural suffix, this structure is marked as unusual:

Are you the e e cummings?

We've got a lot of Hayleys in Year 9.

The status of the relatively new word *internet* is interesting. My computer signals a mistake if I do not use a capital letter, but lower case is often used in the media, for example. Although it rarely occurs in a plural form, it is usually preceded by the definite article. Perhaps it depends on the attitude of the writer: 'the Internet' is special and unique in the eyes of Microsoft, but on a par with 'the library' for journalists and teachers?

Count v. mass nouns

Five items or less	or	*Five items or fewer.*
My sister has brown hairs	or	*My sister has brown hair.*
I don't like fishes	or	*I don't like fish.*

The distinction between these sub-classes of nouns can be used to explain some differences between standard and non-standard English, such as the examples above.

One way of explaining the difference between count and mass nouns is based on *meaning*. **Count nouns**, as the name suggests, are said to refer to things that can be counted. **Mass nouns** are sometimes called 'uncountable', as they refer to entities regarded as a single unit. This distinction is not always a matter of common sense. Try dividing the following words into those that can be counted and those that cannot:

money, cash, wage, coin, loaf, bread, fish, hair.

A definition based on meaning would include 'money' and 'cash' as things that can be counted, yet they do not belong to the class of count nouns.

Insertion test

A more reliable definition is based on *form*. Count nouns can take a plural form; mass nouns cannot.

 Go to www.routledge.com/cw/ross for Activity 5.8, Using the insertion test, to identify mass and count nouns. **Y10+**

Applications to standard and non-standard English

Mass and count nouns can also be distinguished by the ways they *function* in relation to other words. The previous activities showed that common nouns are generally preceded by determiners, such as 'the' and 'a'. There are some differences in the determiners used before mass and count nouns.

> *How <u>much</u> cash is there?*   *How <u>many</u> coins are there?*
>
> *There is <u>less</u> cash now.*   *There are <u>fewer</u> coins now.*

Language users rarely confuse *much* and *many*, but the distinction between *less* and *fewer* is disappearing in contemporary English. The following examples are both considered non-standard:

> *There is too much exams these days.*
>
> *School pupils will take less exams in the revised curriculum.*

Perhaps only the first example struck you as 'ungrammatical'. The second example is becoming so common in contemporary use that it may soon be accepted as standard. Sir Mike Tomlinson, (former Chief Inspector for Education) used the phrase 'less exams' in place of the standard 'fewer exams' in an interview on Radio 4. The few people that noticed phoned in to complain about his 'incorrect' grammar.

Although most people do not 'know or care about' this aspect of grammar, teachers might like to be aware of the changing use and attitudes. Supermarket checkout counters provide evidence of this. It is common to find signs reading:

> *Nine items or less*

but there is some variation, depending on the company and its location. Marks & Spencer, for example, used the standard form:

> *5 items or fewer (observed in 1994)*

but, in its stores in Sheffield, it has changed to the more common use of:

Five items or less

However, the standard version was still used in the south of England. We can see that the standard form retains its prestige, but the distinction is rarely observed, except in the most formal situations. **N.B.** Supermarkets now avoid this pitfall. There is now a checkout for 'Baskets Only'.

Concrete v abstract nouns

In this distinction, the differences in *meaning* are fundamental. **Abstract nouns** refer to qualities or states; **concrete nouns** refer to material entities that can be perceived by the five senses.

 Go to www.routledge.com/cw/ross for Activity 5.9, Distinguishing between abstract and concrete nouns. **Y10+**

Form

Many abstract nouns can be recognised by their morphology. They are often derived from adjectives, and other nouns, using these suffixes:

child	+	*hood*
scholar	+	*ship*
free	+	*dom*
dull	+	*ness*
classic	+	*ism*
pedestrian	+	*isation*

Applications to style and levels of formality

The use of abstract nouns is a feature of many formal types of writing. The term **nominalisation** is used to describe the process of using a verb as a noun – generally an abstract noun. This change of word class can happen in three ways:

1. The noun may be formed by the addition of a suffix:

    You must *behave*.   (verb)   Your *behaviour* is bad. (noun)

2. There may be an internal change to the form of the word:

    I want to *choose*.   (verb)   Give me a *choice*.   (noun)

3. The change in word class may not involve any change in the form of the word:

    We need to *change*. (verb)   *Change* is vital.   (noun)

This term, nominalisation, is used in the Key Stage Framework to identify a common feature of formal writing. For example, verbs in the first sentence are changed to nouns in the second:

1.   *We have <u>decided</u> not to <u>begin liaising</u> with community groups.*

2.   *We have taken the <u>decision</u> to defer <u>implementation</u> of <u>liaison</u> with community groups.*

 Go to www.routledge.com/cw/ross for Activity 5.10, Identifying and commenting on the use of nominalisation in formal writing. **Y10+**

Reading for implied meaning

The use of abstract nouns, including those formed by nominalisation, is a feature of more formal styles of writing. However, choice of vocabulary might not simply alter the level of formality, but might have more subtle effects on meaning. The linguist Norman Fairclough (2000) suggests that nominalisation implies meanings in persuasive uses of language, such as political texts. He argues that the role of a verb, such as 'exclude', is to refer to a process; for example:

> *The school will exclude disruptive pupils.*

In this structure, information is conveyed about who performs the action, who is affected and when it happens. In contrast, the role of a noun, such as 'exclusion', is to refer to a state:

> *We maintain a policy of exclusion.*

This structure backgrounds details of the process and foregrounds the positive outcome. Fairclough (ibid.) shows that many political documents prefer the use of a noun to a verb. For example:

> In the first leaflet produced by the Social Exclusion Unit, the verb *exclude* is used only once, whereas the nominalisation *exclusion* occurs fifteen times.
>
> (Fairclough, 2000)

Although these examples are more appropriate to undergraduate study, they demonstrate how a straightforward 'naming of parts' may be developed into revealing analysis of ways meanings are implied in texts.

 Go to www.routledge.com/cw/ross for Activity 5.11, Analysing the use of nominalisation in a political speech. **Y12+**

Use of concrete and abstract nouns

In many texts, there is a mixture of abstract and concrete nouns. Pupils should be able to identify the types of nouns used and then comment on the effect.

 Go to www.routledge.com/cw/ross for Activity 5.12, Analysing the use of abstract and common nouns in a political speech. **Y10+**

Nouns in summary

TABLE 5.2 Nouns summary

Function	generally preceded by determiners
Form	generally take suffixes '–s', '–'s'. addition of certain suffixes changes other word classes to nouns
Meaning	refer to people, places, institutions, states

The next section on pronouns demonstrates a further way of identifying nouns.

Pronouns

Although native speakers have an intuitive understanding of the role of pronouns, the examples below show some non-standard uses. The ability to identify types of pronoun can be used to explain some differences between standard English and colloquial or dialectal language use. The choice of pronoun can also influence the formality of a text, from impersonal to direct address.

Glossary
pronoun   personal   possessive   reflexive   indefinite   interrogative   relative

What's tha (thou) done?

I'll give thee a clue.

Me and my friend went shopping.

It is I, (or) It is me.

Who did you see? (or) Whom did you see?

I hate football, me.

It was enjoyed by myself.

He did it hisself.

When meeting a lady, one should doff one's cap.

If anyone wishes to apply for the post, they should send their CV.

It was her what did it.

hi there, i got your email...

What is a pronoun?

This is straightforward in many ways. As the label suggests, pronouns *function* in the place of nouns. The *meaning* is simple to explain: pronouns refer to people (or animals, or things). Like all closed classes, membership of this class is finite. All the pronouns in the English language could be listed, in theory: 'I', 'me', 'mine', 'myself', 'someone', 'who', etc.

The *form* of pronouns is relatively complex, as the glossary of terms suggests. Unlike other languages, modern English no longer has many inflections on nouns, adjectives and verbs. Pronouns still change their form, however, to indicate person, possession and case (whether subject or object of a verb).

 Go to www.routledge.com/cw/ross for Activity 5.13, Using pupils' intuitive grasp of pronoun use in English. **Y7+**

Applications to style and levels of formality

The examples at the beginning of the section showed some variations between standard and non-standard uses of English. These differences can be identified and explained, using the terminology for pronouns.

Personal pronoun: Second person

> *What's tha (thou) done?*
>
> *I'll give thee a clue.*

There have been some changes to the pronoun system of English over time. Many languages still have a distinction between a formal and informal address to another person, e.g.: *tu* v. *vous*, in French. The older distinction between 'thee' and 'thou' has disappeared from contemporary English, but traces of it remain in some regional dialects. The standard English 'you' is appropriate for formal speaking and writing, with the dialect forms used in colloquial speech, or for dialogue in plays or narratives.

Personal pronoun: 1st person forms

Me and my friend went shopping.

Personal pronouns are still inflected to indicate case (subject or object). Although 'Me went shopping' is clearly ungrammatical, the non-standard form is often used in longer subject groups, such as 'Me and my friend' above.
The colloquial use of 'me' has become so common that the standard form:

My friend and I went shopping

may seem over-formal in speech. However, pupils should learn that it is appropriate in formal styles of writing.
This has lead to some other changes in pronoun use. Prescriptive grammars, based on Latin would say that the verb 'to be' is not followed by an object, thus the 'correct' form would be:

It is I.   rather than   *It is me.*

Yet the latter structure is used so widely that the former seems hyper-correct. The distinction between 'who' and 'whom' is also rarely observed in contemporary language use:

Who did you see?

is such a common structure that may be considered standard use, with:

Whom did you see?

only used in the most formal types of writing.

Reflexive pronouns

Reflexive pronouns are used with certain verbs to refer back to the subject:

I washed / enjoyed myself.

They can also be used at the end of the structure for emphasis:

I enjoy football, myself.

The non-standard variation uses the personal pronoun instead:

I hate football, me.

The reverse – also non-standard – happens in attempts to sound formal:

It was enjoyed by myself.

The dialect forms of reflexive pronouns are interesting, as an aspect of language change:

He did it hisself. They did it theirselves.

Although regarded as non-standard, they actually follow a regular pattern that may once have been standard.

I	*me*	***my***	*myself*	
you	*you*	***your***	*yourself*	
she	*her*	***her***	*herself*	
he	*<u>him</u>*	***his***	*hisself*	*himself*
we	*us*	***our***	*ourselves*	
they	*<u>them</u>*	***their***	*theirselves*	*themselves*

Impersonal pronouns

The pronoun system of English lacks an accepted way of referring to people in general. The impersonal pronoun 'one' is restricted to the most formal speaking and writing situations.

> *When meeting a lady, one should doff one's cap.*

There is no singular pronoun in the English language that includes both genders. This causes problems of style, if the writer intends a general reference.

> *If anyone wishes to apply for the post, they should send their CV.*

It used to be acceptable to use the pronoun *he* to refer to both males and females. This is no longer the case, as it is misleadingly exclusive.

> *If a pupil arrives late,* he *should report to the office.*

Some solutions are clumsy:

> *If a pupil arrives late,* he or she *should report to the office.*

The shorthand solution is sometimes used:

> *If a pupil arrives late,* s/he *should report to the office.*

The use of 'they' avoids being gender-specific, but risks the charge of being inconsistent, as it uses a plural term to refer to a singular 'person' or 'anyone'.

> *If anyone arrives late,* they *should report to the office.*

However, many people accept this use today, as the lesser of two evils.

Relative pronouns

> *It was her what did it.*

The term relative pronoun is used for words that function as connectives between phrases or clauses.

> *I met the person* <u>who</u> *wanted to buy my TV.*
>
> *I met the person* <u>whom</u> *(? who) you recommended.*

(See page 45 on subordinating conjunctions and Chapter 10 on sentences).

I bought the TV	*<u>which</u> you recommended.*
I bought the TV	*<u>that</u> you recommended.*
I bought the TV	*[ ] you recommended.*
I bought the TV	*<u>what</u> you recommended.*

Standard English uses 'who' or 'whom' to refer back to a person and 'which' to refer to a thing. 'That' can be used for either, and can sometimes be omitted in English structure. Colloquial uses of 'what', as a relative pronoun, are considered non-standard, so should not be used in formal situations.

Personal pronouns: use of capital letters

> *hi there i got your email*

Unlike other languages, English distinguishes the 1st person with a capital letter. We may wonder why reference to self is accorded special status, but it remains the standard form, with some variation in use. Forms of electronic communication often omit capital letters, but pupils should use the standard form for most types of writing.

Applications to style and formality

The choice of pronouns also affects the level of formality. A direct address from 'I', the writer, to 'you', the reader, is appropriate in personal forms of writing.

More formal texts, such as essays and reports, are conventionally impersonal in tone, so tend to avoid such personal reference. At one time, it was an absolute rule that the first and second person 'I' and 'you' should be avoided in essays and reports. However, this convention is now open to debate. Some people feel that it is both clumsy and misleading to rephrase a personal statement:

> *I think that…*   *It is clear that…*

The use of *we* to mean *I* is no longer generally accepted:

> *We will examine the choice of vocabulary.*

It is still agreed that the reader should not be addressed directly as 'you' in essays and reports:

> *If you think about it, …*

 Go to www.routledge.com/cw/ross for Activity 5.14, Exploring the effect of pronoun use on levels of formality. **Y10+**

Applications to style

Pronouns can be used in place of nouns (or noun phrases) to avoid unnecessary repetition. Sometimes, however, pronoun use can cause ambiguity.

In spoken language, pronouns tend to be used more often, as their reference may be made clear by the context. Pupils should be aware of this difference between spoken and written language. Written language does not provide such contextual clues, so more use of nouns is needed, if the writer wishes the meaning to be explicit.

 Go to www.routledge.com/cw/ross for Activity 5.15, Exploring the stylistic effects of pronoun use. **Y7+**

Pronoun Summary

TABLE 5.3 Pronouns summary

Function	can replace nouns, or noun phrases
Form	change to show number, possession, case, etc.
Meaning	refer to people, animals or things

The next chapter looks at the remaining content classes: verbs, adjectives and adverbs.

6

Verbs, adjectives and adverbs

The final chapter on word classes explores the role of verbs, adjectives and adverbs. As with all the other word classes, the familiar definition based on meaning is developed by concentrating on the function of each type of word. Activities use the four tests to develop pupils' understanding of the recommended terminology for these word classes. This knowledge is applied to awareness of language variation and change, including differences between standard and non-standard English; and degrees of formality. Verbs play more complex roles than other word classes, changing form in several ways to express a variety of meanings. The terminology for classifying types of verbs is extensive and may become daunting. For this reason, it is introduced in stages.

In this chapter, the first section introduces some key terms for describing forms of main verbs. Chapter 8 on verb phrases introduces the distinction between a main and an auxiliary verb, with examples of different verb aspects, moods and voices. The distinction between finite and non-finite verbs is illustrated in Chapter 10 on sentence structure.

Verbs

> Prince Harry was monstered by paparazzi.
>
> They papped him.
>
> Chris Ewbank trousered over £20,000.
>
> It can't magic up greater numbers of specialist teachers.
>
> Stop iffing and butting.

How can pupils develop their ability to identify verbs in creative uses of language, such as the examples above? Like all word classes, a verb is fundamentally defined by its role, or function, but may also be explained by its meaning and form.

Glossary

verb	infinitive	tense	present v. past	regular v. irregular
person 1st v 2nd v. 3rd	singular v. plural	present participle/past participle

What is a verb?

The familiar definition is based on meaning: 'a **verb** is a doing word.' This may help to identify those verbs that express actions, but many verbs are not obviously 'doing' anything. The first examples above from newspaper reports might suggest actions, even though 'monster', 'papparazzi' (papped), 'trouser', and 'magic' are more familiar as nouns. But, in the fourth example of 'iffing' and 'butting', the problem is that the person is avoiding doing anything.

Many verbs express *states* rather than actions: 'know', 'belong', 'seem', etc. This is true of the most common verb in English. The verb 'to be' is rarely recognised, if the notion of 'doing word' is used. As it is highly irregular, changing its form in many ways, it should be learnt as a special case.

To be

am	*was*	*been*
is		
are	*were*	*being*

Substitution test

The most reliable ways of identifying verbs is by their function. At this stage, the substitution test can be introduced. If a word can be substituted by a known verb, this suggests it has the role of verb.

Prince Harry was <u>monstered</u> by paparazzi.	*pestered*
They <u>papped</u> him.	*photographed*
Chris Ewbank <u>trousered</u> over £20,000.	*earned*
It can't <u>magic up</u> greater numbers of specialist teachers.	*create*
Stop <u>iffing and butting.</u>	*dithering*

Form

Understanding the form of verbs provides a useful tool. Nouns can change form by the addition of suffixes to show plurals and possession. Verbs also change form to show who and when. The terms for these aspects are **person** and **tense**. The forms of modern English verbs are simple compared to many other languages that use a different form for each person in many tenses. Pupils' intuitive understanding of changes in form and function of English verbs can be used in activities such as the following. Invent a verb (e.g. 'gurn') or take an example of a verb formed from a noun, (e.g. 'leg it', 'belly-ache') and show how it can be used in different forms. For example:

We were legging it.
Don't belly-ache all the time.

Go to www.routledge.com/cw/ross for Activity 6.1, Creating and analysing new verb forms. **Y8+**

Applications to standard and non-standard varieties

It is useful to be aware of a number of common differences between standard English and dialectal variations. Subject-verb agreement in English is simple, compared to other languages, as there is only one change in form. In the simple present tense, the third person takes an *-s* suffix, with some variation in Black English Vernacular:

He go to the café most days.

New verb forms, used in the previous activity, always follow regular structures. However, verbs in common use tend to become irregular. The changes occur in the forms of the past tense, with two distinct forms for the simple past and the past participle. For example:

verb	past tense	past participle
go	*went*	*(have) gone*
see	*saw*	*(have) seen*
do	*did*	*(have) done*

Although these complex verb forms are usually used effortlessly by native speakers, there are some differences between standard and non-standard, or dialect forms of English, such as:

I done it.

I seen it.

In these examples, the past participle has been used instead of the simple past form. The reverse happens in some non-standard uses of verbs:

Have you took my pen?

I've wrote the essay.

This variation occurs with a group of verbs that share similar forms:

present	past	past participle
write	*wrote*	*written*
take	*took*	*taken*
give	*gave*	*given*
drive	*drove*	*driven*
eat	*ate*	*eaten*
show	*showed*	*shown*
get	*got*	*gotten*

N.B. The verb 'to get' is of particular interest, as it indicates that the language may be changing in this respect. There is variation between standard American English and standard British English:

I have gotten.   *I have got.*

Although standard English no longer uses the *-en* suffix for the past participle of this particular verb, all the others in the group follow the *-en* pattern.

The non-standard forms are becoming common in language use – the Google search engine reveals more than 26,000 'hits' for the phrase 'I have wrote' alone. However, pupils should be aware of the difference between these standard and non-standard forms, so that they can use standard English in formal situations.

 Go to www.routledge.com/cw/ross for Activity 6.2, Identifying non-standard verb forms. **Y9+**

Forming nouns and adjectives from verbs

One way of identifying verbs is by their form: the suffixes *-ing*, *-ed*. However, this is not always a reliable way of identifying verbs. Many adjectives are formed from verbs by the addition of these suffixes:

This is <u>boring</u>.   *I feel <u>bored</u>.*

You are <u>annoying</u>.   *I feel <u>annoyed</u>.*

There was a <u>roaring</u> scream as the twister completed its <u>plummeting</u> descent.

Nouns can also be formed from verbs by adding an *-ing* suffix:

<u>Smoking</u> is prohibited.

<u>Drinking</u> is on the increase.

<u>Over-eating</u> leads to obesity.

(See page 71–73 on adjectives).

Substitution test

The substitution test shows whether a particular word – or letter string – functions as a verb, adjective or noun, if it can be replaced by a more familiar word from that class. For example:

I feel annoyed / happy.   *(adjective)*

I annoyed / met my parents.   *(verb)*

Drinking / crime is on the increase.   *(noun)*

She was drinking / making coffee.   *(verb)*

A further substitution test for nouns is to see whether the word can be replaced by a pronoun:

> *Drinking/it is on the increase.* (noun)

Nonsense rhymes can be used to practice identifying the role of word classes. The following Activity uses a parody of Lewis Carroll's poem, 'Jabberwocky'.

 Go to www.routledge.com/cw/ross for Activity 6.3, Identifying verbs by their form: the suffixes used. **Y10+**

The following summary applies to main verbs. Chapter 8 will provide further understanding of the role of verbs in phrases, introducing the concepts of auxiliary verb; perfect and continuous aspects; passive and active voice; indicative, imperative, conditional and subjunctive mood.

Verb summary

TABLE 6.1 Main verbs summary

Function	can be replaced by other verbs
Form	take suffixes, such as '–s', '–ing', '–ed'
Meaning	express actions or states

The next section deals with the remaining content classes: adjectives and adverbs.

Adjectives and adverbs

Adjectives and adverbs can be explored together, as they are similar in some important ways. They are – nearly always – optional elements in the structure of sentences. Because of this, these two word classes are significant for style.

Glossary

adjective   comparative and superlative   adverb   intensifier

---

I notice that you use plain, simple language, short words and brief sentences. That is the way to write English – it is the modern way and the best way. Stick to it; don't let fluff and flowers and verbosity creep in. When you catch an adjective, kill it. No, I don't mean utterly, but kill most of them – then the rest will be valuable. They weaken when they are close together. They give strength when they are wide apart. An adjective habit, or a wordy, diffuse, flowery habit, once fastened upon a person, is as hard to get rid of as any other vice.

(Mark Twain, letter, 1880)

> *If it is possible to cut a word out, always cut it out.*
>
> *(George Orwell*, Politics and the English Language*)*

As pupils develop their repertoire, the use of adjectives and adverbs can create more elaborate ways of expressing themselves in writing. However, experienced writers, like Mark Twain and George Orwell above, often advise restraint in the use of such optional extras. When redrafting descriptive writing, pupils could check for over-use of adjectives in particular. Some may be redundant; the use of well-chosen verbs or nouns can also convey vivid description. First, pupils need ways of identifying adjectives and adverbs. This section will follow a similar approach, exploring the usefulness of definitions based on meaning, form and function.

What is an adjective?

The familiar *meaning* definition of an adjective is 'a describing word'. This is not reliable, as the example in the introduction shows:

> *The drunk tottered into the alley clutching a whisky bottle under his raincoat.*

There are no adjectives in this sentence, but description is provided by nouns such as 'drunk' and 'alley' and the verbs 'tottered' and 'clutching'.

It is more useful to concentrate on the *function* of adjectives in relation to other words in the structure. Adjectives provide more detail about nouns. In English structure, adjectives generally operate in two positions:

> *before nouns*
>
> *after verbs expressing states: to be, to seem, etc.*

Another feature of adjectives is that more than one can be used in a list. The number is infinite in theory, but limited by considerations of style.

Insertion test

The insertion test can be used to collect a store of familiar adjectives in these two positions in English structure.

 Go to www.routledge.com/cw/ross for Activity 6.4, Introducing a reliable way of identifying adjectives. **Y7+**

Substitution test

Pupils can use their store of known-adjectives substitution tests to check the role of apparently 'descriptive' words.

 Go to www.routledge.com/cw/ross for Activity 6.5, The ways the – apparently – same word can function as different word classes. **Y10+**

Deletion test

The deletion test is the most useful way of identifying adjectives. As adjectives are optional elements, they can often be removed without destroying the structure. Those [lazy, hazy] days of summer.

N.B. Remember that adverbs are also optional extras. Further tests are needed to distinguish these two word classes.

 Go to www.routledge.com/cw/ross for Activity 6.6, Identifying adjectives by using the deletion test, followed by the substitution test. **Y10+**

Form

Pupils' knowledge of morphology can be used to identify adjectives. Certain suffixes indicate a change from noun or verb to adjective:

	noun	*adjective*
–ious	caution	caut*ious*
–ful	beauty	beauti*ful*
–ent	intelligence	intellig*ent*
–al	person	person*al*
–y	wind	wind*y*

Other suffixes indicate a change from verb to adjective.

	verb	*adjective*
–ing	annoy	annoy*ing*
–ed	bore	bor*ed*

Adjectives themselves can change form in two ways to show comparative and superlative.

The suffix –er is added to some adjectives to compare their quality with another:

This car is bigger than the one I usually drive.

The suffix –est is added if more than two things are compared.

This is the biggest car I have ever driven.

This knowledge of the form of adjectives can be used in an insertion test. An unfamiliar word, such as 'slithy' or 'mimsy' from 'The Jabberwocky' (Lewis Carroll), can take the comparative and superlative form: 'slithier' or 'mimsiest'.

Applications to standard English

There are, of course, exceptions to these two rules that cause some non-standard forms of adjectives. For example:

> *gooder, bestest, beautifullest, most favouritest, more harder, deader*

Pupils should be aware of the exceptions to the rule. Two common adjectives are irregular:

> *good, better, best; bad, worse, worst.*

Adjectives with more than two syllables generally use 'more' or 'most' in place of a suffix:

> *more beautiful, most favourite*

Adjectives do not take both a suffix and a modifier:

> either *more lovely* or *lovelier*

Some adjectives cannot be compared, because of their meaning:

> *dead, pregnant, perfect,* etc.

Application to style

As adjectives are optional extras in English structure, it is a matter of stylistic choice. In descriptive writing, pupils learn to use adjectives to add effective detail. However, they should be aware that a plain style may also be effective. Writers may also convey a vivid scene by the use of effective nouns and verbs.

 Go to www.routledge.com/cw/ross for Activity 6.7, Discussing stylistic variation and the effect of using more/fewer adjectives. **Y12+**

Adjective summary

TABLE 6.2 Adjectives summary

Function	can be inserted before nouns, or after stative verbs more than one can be inserted in these positions can often be deleted
Form	can take a comparative or superlative form certain suffixes indicate a change in word class to adjectives
Meaning	add detail to the noun

Adverbs

Adverbs are the most varied and flexible of the word classes, performing a range of functions. The familiar definition of an adverb refers to both its meaning and its function: 'an adverb describes a verb and tells you how, when or where it happened'. It is true that adverbs often function with verbs, but they have another important role in English structure – adverbs also function to qualify adjectives or other adverbs. Pupils should become aware that, as optional extras, adverbs have an effect on style.

Glossary
adverb   connective   intensifier

> *What would make 2005 a good year for you and your school?*
>
> *I'm not looking forward to 2005 too much because I've got my GCSEs. My big hope is that they go well. I'm a bit dodgy on subjects like French: too many genders, too many accents. But my maths and sciences aren't bad and I'd really like good grades for those. It would be nice if our football team could win a bit more often. We aren't bad, but we could do with more practice. That might make a difference. If we could have a new sports stadium with a pool and a gym, that would be pretty good too, but it won't happen because there's no space and I shouldn't think there's any money, either.*
>
> *(Jamie Bird, 15, London, writing in* The Guardian*)*

The over-use of adverbs, particularly the colloquial 'just' and 'really', is a common feature of pupils' writing. The above example uses many adverbs, which are effective in conveying the personal feelings of the writer in a spontaneous, informal way. In more formal situations, however, the writer might remove the impressionistic adverbs: 'too much', 'bit', 'really', 'pretty'. In order to make these choices, pupils should be able to identify adverbs.

What is an adverb?

Adverbs are closely related to adjectives in *form*, as many adverbs are formed by adding the suffix *–ly* to an adjective:

> *warmly, independently, graciously, thankfully, really*

In these cases, it is straightforward to identify adverbs by their form. However, many adverbs do not have this recognisable form:

> *now, just, hard, very, always, too, so*

The common definition refers to the *meaning* of adverbs – to provide more information about the verb: where, when or how it happened. But there are many exceptions to this. Exploring the ways adverbs *function* is the most reliable.

Deletion and transposition tests

Like adjectives, adverbs are optional elements in the structure, so can be deleted. The unique feature of adverbs, however, is their moveability. Adverbs can be moved to various positions in English structure:

- immediately before the verb;
- after the verb;
- between parts of the verb phrase;
- at the beginning of the structure;
- at the end of the structure.

> [*Stealthily*] a figure [*stealthily*] was [*stealthily*] approaching [*stealthily*].

These features of adverbs are shown in the following activity, which returns to the extract used to identify adjectives.

Go to www.routledge.com/cw/ross for Activity 6.8, Discussing stylistic variation and the effect of using more/fewer adverbs. **Y12+**

Transposition

Many adverbs do not have the easily recognisable form – the suffix *-ly*. The transposition test is a reliable way of checking whether a word functions as an adverb. (If the word can be deleted, it could be an adjective or adverb.) The meaning definition can be used to support this conclusion.

Go to www.routledge.com/cw/ross for Activity 6.9, Showing a reliable way to identify adverbs. **Y7+**

Applications to style

The previous activities showed the way adverbs can function to add detail about the time, place or manner of the action described by the verb. However, another important function of adverbs is as **connectives**, providing links between sentences. One example is the word 'however' used in the previous sentence. Other adverbs – and adverbial phrases – are commonly used to maintain the cohesion of a text. Like conjunctions, these adverbs express various relationships between sentences.

(See Chapter 13 on Discourse).

TABLE 6.3 Adverbs summary

Addition	also, furthermore, moreover
Opposition	however, nevertheless, instead, on the other hand
Reinforcing	besides, anyway, after all
Explaining	for example, in other words, that is to say
Listing	first(ly), next, finally
Indicating result	therefore, consequently, as a result
Indicating time	just then, meanwhile, later

Another function of adverbs is to indicate the point of view of the writer or speaker.

We will <u>hopefully</u> get tickets for Glastonbury.

Some people object to this use of adverbs, as they do not qualify the verb – it is not the getting of tickets that is hopeful, but the feelings of the speaker. It is clearer to use these adverbs at the beginning or end of the structure:

<u>Allegedly</u>, the accused purchased the Rolex from a market stall.

Although considered non-standard by some, this use of adverbs is common, even in more formal writing. This makes adverbs highly significant in implying meanings. The ability to identify adverbs can help pupils distinguish impersonal statements from expression of personal attitudes.

 Go to www.routledge.com/cw/ross for Activity 6.10, Identifying adverbs that express the writer's attitudes. **Y12+**

Insertion test

Although adverbs of time and place can provide precise details, adverbs of manner often express personal opinions. For this reason, they are often omitted from texts with a formal, objective or authoritative tone, such as religious, academic, scientific or legal language. The effect on style can be shown, using the insertion test with colloquial adverbs.

 Go to www.routledge.com/cw/ross for Activity 6.11, Exploring the effect of adverbs on the formality of texts. **Y12+**

Adverbs used with adjectives

Although the term 'adverb' suggests its role with verbs, adverbs are also commonly used to modify adjectives. The term **intensifier** is often used for this function of adverbs. This is because they usually express the degree – or intensity – of the adjective.

The handwriting was	*barely*	*legible.*
	fairly	
	quite	
	reasonably	
	perfectly	

Adverbs can also occur before other adverbs, performing a similar function:

Please write	*very*	*legibly.*

In the examples above, intensifiers were used to differentiate degrees of legibility. Often, however, intensifiers do not convey anything precise or objective. They express a vague sense of emphasis, so are more common in colloquial speech than in writing. The choice of a particular intensifier tends to reflect the social identity of the writer or speaker: 'That was well good.'

 Go to www.routledge.com/cw/ross for Activity 6.12, Exploring the function and stylistic effect of adverbs used as intensifiers. **Y8+**

Summary adverbs

TABLE 6.4 Adverbs summary

Function	can occur with verbs – can be deleted or transposed
	can occur before adjectives or other adverbs – can be deleted
Form	may be formed by adding the suffix '–ly' to adjectives
Meaning	express meanings such as time, place and manner with verbs
	express degrees of intensity with adjectives

7

Noun phrases

The next two chapters move up to the third level of structure – the way words combine to form phrases.

TABLE 7.1 Levels of structure

One or more **morphemes**	combine to form	words.
One or more **words**	combine to form	phrases.
One or more **phrases**	combine to form	clauses.
One or more **clauses**	combine to form	sentences.
One or more **sentences**	combine to form	paragraphs and whole texts.

In some ways, the best starting point for grammar study is with phrases, as this is where the structure of language becomes obvious. A sentence may look like a chain of individual words on the surface, but is, in fact, a more complex three-dimensional structure. As the examples in the Introduction showed, phrases (and clauses) are often embedded beneath the surface. These two sentences have the same underlying structure of four phrases.

> *Teenagers / upset / me / now.*
>
> *[The rowdy behaviour of teenage children] [has been upsetting]*
> *[the whole family] [for the past year].*

The term 'phrase' suggests a group of words, but it is more helpful to think of a phrase as a unit. Like a family, a phrase may consist of a single member – word – but can expand to include related elements within the unit. So the single noun 'teenagers' is expanded into a longer phrase: 'the rowdy behaviour of teenagers'.

Just as market research uses the concept of the 'head' of the household, phrases are classified according to the headword. There are five types of phrases, each associated with the content word classes: noun, verb, adjective and adverb, as well as preposition phrases. The example above uses:

TABLE 7.2

Noun phrases	the rowdy *behaviour* of teenagers
	the whole *family*
Verb phrase	has been *upsetting*
Prepositional phrase	*for* the past year

Study of phrase structure helps to consolidate pupils' understanding of the role of word classes: nouns are usually grouped with determiners and adjectives; main verbs often occur with auxiliary verbs.

Phrases are a significant feature of language variation. Awareness of simple and complex phrases can be applied to reading skills. Pupils should notice how some writers of fiction use a plain style, whereas others employ more detailed description. The use of complex noun phrases is a feature of formal, academic styles – more so than the use of complex sentence structures. This awareness can be applied to pupils' own writing, as they are often explicitly rewarded in mark schemes for the use of more complex phrases.

Pupils also need to develop their ability to use a range of verb phrases to express various aspects of time in narratives. Writing to persuade often involves expression of hypothetical or suggested ideas. In English grammar, aspects of time, conditional and subjunctive meanings are expressed by the expansion of the verb phrase, (rather than the many different verb endings used in Romance languages).

This chapter deals with noun, preposition, adjective and adverb phrases. Chapter 8 explores verb phrases.

Noun phrase structure

This section explores the structure of noun phrases, beginning with the basic element of a single noun and showing the ways this can be expanded by the insertion of other elements. These may be single words – determiners and adjectives – as Chapter 6 showed. But more complex noun phrases are formed by adding other phrases, or even clauses.

Glossary
noun   phrase   headword   modifier   post-modification   prepositional phrase

ANGST-RIDDEN MELODIC SCREAMY METAL-CORE.

(flyer advertising a music gig)

> *Hydroterapia Detoxifying Moisturised Sea Salts*
>
> > (product name/label on bottle)
>
> *Bargain sofa hunters. If you missed the DFS December Sale, Double Discount Boxing Day Sale, January Clearance Sale and the February End of Winter Sale, don't worry – the Spring Sale starts in March.*
>
> > (Parody of sales' promotions in Viz)

The most simple **noun phrase** is a single noun. In the examples above, the key nouns are:

> *metal-core, salts, sale*

The term **headword** is used in many grammar books to refer to the essential role of this key element of each phrase.

As the examples above of promotional language show, the noun phrase can be expanded to provide more precise, enticing details. The bottle, for example, does not simply contain *salts*, but a particular – even unique – product:

> sea <u>salts</u>
>
> moisturised sea <u>salts</u>
>
> detoxifying moisturised sea <u>salts</u>
>
> Hydroterapia   detoxifying moisturised sea <u>salts</u>

All three examples use this structure of noun phrases: the insertion of words *before* the noun.

Insertion test

 Go to www.routledge.com/cw/ross for Activity 7.1, Using the insertion test to show the type of words that can be used to expand noun phrases. **Y7+**

Noun phrases as titles

Noun phrases usually occur as part of full sentence structures, but it is helpful to look first at examples of noun phrases in isolation. Brand names provide a source of useful, contemporary examples: titles of films, books and TV programmes; names of products, bands, clubs, restaurants etc. These are generally quite 'snappy', but people can go to absurd lengths creating impressive job titles. This example from Essex County Council was held up to ridicule in the media:

> *Decriminalisation of Parking Enforcement Project Implementation Manager.*
>
> > (Daily Mail, *16 February 2005*)

In the classroom, book titles can be used to consolidate pupils' awareness of noun phrase structure. Many follow the basic structure illustrated above: the headword alone, or preceded by determiners and/or modifiers:

> *Holes*
>
> *The <u>Odyssey</u>*
>
> *Good <u>Bones</u>*
>
> *The Wrong <u>Boy</u>*
>
> *The No. 1 Ladies Detective <u>Agency</u>*

Go to www.routledge.com/cw/ross for Activity 7.2, For examples of titles of horror stories with this noun phrase structure. **Y7+**

Go to www.routledge.com/cw/ross for Activity 7.3, To consolidate awareness of this structure by creating book titles. **Y7+**

Applications to style

Pupils are assessed for their ability to use more complex noun phrases. This is often done in descriptive writing by the addition of one or more adjectives before the headword. For example:

> *black <u>clothes</u>*
>
> *the cold, frosty <u>air</u>*
>
> *Avril, a stupid immature <u>girl</u>*
>
> *an evil-looking and rather scary <u>poodle</u>*

They should be aware, however, that a plain style may also be effective.

Go to www.routledge.com/cw/ross for Activity 7.4, Showing the stylistic effects of two different styles of narrative. **Y12+**

Expanding noun phrases after the headword

So far, we have looked at noun phrases with all the extra detail inserted before the key noun. The other way of expanding noun phrases is by adding detail after the noun. Some grammar books use the term **post-modification** for this structure. In the structure of some languages, it is common to place adjectives after the noun, but this is very rare in English grammar. The few examples are often influenced by French.

> *<u>heir</u> apparent*
>
> *Little <u>boy</u> blue*

The following examples were used in an airline magazine, but the writer is not a native speaker of English:

> It is a journey *strange* and a journey *bold*. But be assured it will be a journey *magical*.
>
> (*Heinz Gerhardt, RA.M editorial*)

The use of this unusual structure tends to draw attention to itself – it is stylistically marked. The opening sentence of *Pride and Prejudice* (Jane Austen) provides a well-known example:

> It is a <u>truth</u>, *universally acknowledged that a single man, in possession of a large fortune, must be in want of a wife.*

The usual structure would be:

> *It is a universally acknowledged* <u>truth</u>*...*

If an adjective is placed after the noun, it is usually part of a phrase:

> *The* <u>cup</u>*, full of water.*

It is far more common to use a different form of phrase to add detail after the noun. Examples from the previous extracts follow a similar pattern:

> *the* <u>lights</u> *of the caboose*
> *both* <u>sides</u> *of the track*
> *the* <u>edge</u> *of the track*
> *a strange* <u>air</u> *of ineffectuality*

The type of phrases used in this role are called **prepositional phrases**, because a preposition – *of* – is used to link the key noun with another noun phrase.

Insertion test

 Go to www.routledge.com/cw/ross for Activity 7.5, Creating more complex noun phrases by adding prepositional phrases. **Y7+**

Application to style

Although it often assumed that complex sentence structures are a feature of formal writing, recent research based on a large corpus of texts showed a different type of complexity. Formal writing often uses complex noun phrases within a simple sentence structure. The examples in Activity 7.6 are taken from an academic text on language, and an article written by a 15-year-old boy, who won a place at Cambridge University. The sentence structures are, in fact, quite simple. It is the expanded noun phrases that increase the level of complexity.

 Go to www.routledge.com/cw/ross for Activity 7.6, Analysing complexity of texts at the level of noun phrases. **Y11+**

Using clauses to expand noun phrases

The previous activity showed a further way of expanding noun phrases: by inserting clauses after the key noun:

> *Its efficiency in this role depends on the type of information <u>being conveyed</u>.*
>
> *I remember a feeling <u>which permeated everything</u>.*

Tests

How can we tell that the clause is part of the noun phrase? The tests of deletion, substitution and insertion can be used.

Deletion test: What parts of the structure can be removed, leaving the basic structure intact?

> *Its efficiency in this role depends on the type of information [<u>being conveyed</u>].*
>
> *I remember a feeling [<u>which permeated everything</u>].*

Substitution test: what does the pronoun *it* replace?

> *Its efficiency depends on <u>it</u> [the type of information being conveyed].*
>
> *I remember <u>it</u> [a feeling which permeated everything].*

Although the use of subordinate clauses to expand a noun is a complex structure, it is commonly used and easily understood. Nursery rhymes and children's stories often use this structure:

> *This is the <u>house</u> [that Jack built].*
>
> *This is the <u>rat</u> [that lived in the house that Jack built].*
>
> *This is the <u>cat</u> [that killed the rat that lived in the house that Jack built].*

Insertion test: What words, phrases and clauses can be added to provide more precise detail to the key noun?

 Go to www.routledge.com/cw/ross for Activity 7.7, Creating complex noun phrases for precise description. **Y7+**

Linking clauses to noun phrases

Clauses are linked to the noun phrase by **connectives**. The conjunctions often used in this role are: *which, who, that*.

> *This is the cat <u>which</u> chased the rat.*
>
> *This is the dog <u>who</u> killed the cat.*
>
> *This is the house <u>that</u> Jack built.*

N.B. In English grammar, it is possible to omit the conjunction 'that'.

This is the house [ ] Jack built.

The other way of connecting clauses to the noun is the use of a verb with the suffix *–ing* or *–ed.*

a Playstation equipped with dual control

the information being conveyed

(See Chapter 9 on subordinate clauses).

These verb forms are termed 'non-finite': the present and past 'participle'.

Applications to style

Some genres of writing use highly complex noun phrases for various reasons. Academic, technical or legal texts need to specify details to be as accurate and precise as possible. Advertisements, as seen at the beginning of this section, tend to include details to promote the product as desirable.

 Go to www.routledge.com/cw/ross for Activity 7.8, Analysing the use of noun phrases in the genre of estate agents' leaflets, then creating a similar text. **Y9+**

Noun phrase summary

TABLE 7.3 Noun phrases summary

Substitution	A noun phrase can be replaced by a preposition.
Insertion	A single noun can be expanded in various ways: – determiner and modifiers before the key noun – prepositional phrases after the key noun – clauses after the key noun.
Deletion	Modifiers and postmodifiers can be removed from the structure. Determiners are usually essential and cannot be deleted.

The next section looks at the ways single adjectives and adverbs can be expanded into longer phrases.

Adjectival and adverbial phrases

Adjectival and adverbial phrases are relatively simple in structure. As pupils intuitively use and understand these phrases, it may not be necessary to provide explicit teaching of the forms. Their function may also seem obvious – to provide more detailed description. However, as optional elements, the use of adjectival and adverbial phrases has an effect on style. Pupils should be aware that the use of intensifiers creates a more personal, informal style.

Glossary
adjectival phrase **adverbial phrase** **prepositional phrase** **intensifier**

> But these <u>minor</u> worries could <u>hardly</u> compare with the consternation caused on the Monopoly front by a <u>swift-fingered</u> checker-out from a Bedford supermarket whose palm was <u>so</u> <u>extraordinarily</u> <u>speedy</u> in the recovery of the two dice thrown from the <u>cylindrical</u> cup that her opponents had <u>little</u> option to accept, without ever seeing the <u>slightest</u> evidence, her <u>instantaneously enunciated</u> score, and then to watch <u>helplessly</u> as this <u>sharp-faced</u> woman moved her <u>little</u> counter along the board to whichever square seemed of the <u>greatest potential</u> profit to her <u>entrepeneurial</u> designs.
>
> (The secret of Annexe 3, *a Morse Mystery'*, Colin Dexter, 1986)

The example above uses adjectives and adverbs (underlined) to add descriptive detail to a scene in a novel. Unlike nouns or verbs, they usually occur as a single word:

He watched <u>helplessly</u>.

Form of phrases

There are only a few ways of expanding an adjective or adverb into a longer phrase. This is usually done by inserting words before the headword – pre-modification:

Her palm was [so extraordinarily] <u>speedy</u>.

There are only a few possibilities for post-modification:

Her palm was [very] <u>speedy</u> [indeed].

 Go to www.routledge.com/cw/ross for Activity 7.9, Expanding adjective and adverbial phrases. **Y9+**

Applications to style

The previous activity showed that adjectival and adverbial phrases can be expanded by adding adverbs. In this role, adverbs are sometimes called 'intensifiers', as they indicate how lovely the cat is, or how soundly it sleeps. This is often a matter of style, rather than adding precise information – it would be difficult to say which of the modifiers expressed the highest degree:

very / extremely / really / lovely

As Chapter 6 showed, the use of intensifiers often reflects the speaker's, or writer's, background, as well as their attitude. For this reason, formal texts tend to avoid the use of these modifiers. Experienced writers may use them deliberately to convey an extreme, personal opinion in an informal style.

 Go to www.routledge.com/cw/ross for Activity 7.10, Identifying the use of intensifiers as a marker of informality in journalism. **Y10+**

Adjectival and adverbial phrase summary

TABLE 7.4 Adjectival and adverbial phrases summary

Form	Adverbs can come before the headword.
	A few adverbs can come after the headword.
Function	These optional elements can be deleted.
	The phrase can often be replaced by a single word.
Meaning	The modifiers often 'intensify' the headword.

Chapter 8 explores the remaining type of phrase – the ways a single main verb can be expanded into longer verb phrases to convey a range of meanings.

8

Verb phrases

This chapter explores verb phrases. Because the structure is governed by a few fixed rules, the terminology is more detailed. The shades of meaning conveyed by verb phrases are explained, using the concepts of _tense_, _aspect_, _mood_ and _voice_.

Native language users operate this complex system of verbs intuitively, so teachers need to weigh the benefits of explicit knowledge against the drawbacks of 'too much information'. Even students of EFL or EAL (English as a Foreign Language, or English as an Alternative Language) can acquire a functional use of English without knowing the terms for the structures. Teaching of foreign languages in schools today has also moved away from a structural approach – to the regret of some teachers!

For the sake of 'completeness', I have chosen to cover all the terms and concepts that were used in the National Literacy Strategy, but I am aware that this knowledge was gained over a lifetime. I hope that discerning readers will also make choices – to skip some sections, pick those that seem most useful for their pupils, and use the book for reference as necessary.

Structure of verb phrases

Glossary
main v. auxiliary verb   tense   aspect   mood   voice

> _The kidnappers stalked a local man._
> _Two men were stalking the girl in the park._
> _She had been stalking him for two days._
> _Nadia has been being stalked for the last day or so._
> _You might have been being stalked by agents who just want to offer you membership._

Verb phrase structure is relatively straightforward. The examples above show how a simple verb phrase – _stalked_ – can be expanded by the addition of modifiers. Compared to the flexibility of noun phrases, verb phrase structure is restricted to a few set patterns:

- only verbs can be used as modifiers;
- modifiers always come before the headword;
- the number of modifiers is limited to four;
- the order of modifiers is fixed.

Main v. auxiliary verbs

The patterns above move from the most simple to the most complex structure of verb phrases. The first important distinction is between main and auxiliary verbs. The term **main verb** is used for the key word that conveys the meaning, or content. The term **auxiliary verb** is used for the 'helping', or grammatical words in the structure.

Auxiliary verbs				*Main verbs*
				stalked
			were	*stalking*
		had	*been*	*stalking*
	has	*been*	*being*	*stalked*
might	*have*	*been*	*being*	*stalked*

Most verb functions can be expressed using no more than two auxiliary verbs. The first three combinations are those most frequently used to express present or past events. The final two structures involve the passive voice, with a conditional slant expressed in the most complex verb phrase. The use of four auxiliary verbs is possible in English grammar, but extremely rare in authentic language use.

Insertion test

Pupils' intuitive grasp of the common verb phrase structures can be demonstrated in creative activities. They can be asked to expand any single verb by inserting auxiliary verbs before the main verb.

 Go to www.routledge.com/cw/ross for Activity 8.1, Creating a variety of verb phrases. **Y10+**

Tense

Glossary
tense   present tense   past tense   future   time   non-standard   negatives

The first way of classifying verbs is by **tense**. Unfortunately, this term is not used consistently. A common assumption is that tense is equivalent to time, with the distinction between past, present and future. In that case, there would be three tenses in language. If we turn to grammar texts for an explanation, there are conflicting opinions about the number of tenses in English: some say there are five, others seven, or even 14.

In this book, I use the technical definition: the term 'tense' refers to the distinction between *forms* of the main verb. Some languages, such as French, use different forms of the verb for many different tenses: present, future, past, imperfect, pluperfect, conditional, subjunctive. The English language only changes the form of the main verb to indicate a distinction between present and past tense. So there are two tenses in English:

Past tense	*Present tense*
I came, I saw, I conquered. (past)	*I come, I see, I conquer. (present)*

N.B. Future time is expressed by using auxiliary verbs. For example:

> *I will conquer.*
>
> *I am going to conquer.*

N.B. It is also possible to refer to future time using forms of the present tense, provided there is no ambiguity:

> *Tomorrow we leave for France.*
>
> *We are leaving in the morning.*

Go to www.routledge.com/cw/ross for Activity 8.2, Identifying present and past tenses and exploring the relationship between tense and time. **Y10+**

Applications to style

In a straightforward world, the term 'present tense' would mean that it refers to the present time. However, this is not strictly accurate. The present tense can be used to convey various meanings.

1   The most common function of the simple present tense is to refer to regular events:

> *I love to rise in a summer morn*
>
> *When the birds sing on every tree;*

2   The present tense can also be used to convey a sense of immediacy or timelessness. Oral and written narratives, for example, may use the present tense to recount past events, sometimes referred to as the 'dramatic' present.

So, I go up to the manager and demand my wages. She just gives me the same old excuses.

N.B. Omission of *–s* for third person is an indication of a dialectal variation, in this case Black English Vernacular (BEV):

One bright Sunday morning in July I <u>have</u> trouble with my Notting Hill landlord because he <u>ask</u> for a month's rent in advance.

(*Jean Rhys*, Let Them Call it Jazz)

3. Newspaper headlines may also use the present tense for past events.

Nelson Mandela <u>speaks</u> to the crowd in Trafalgar Square yesterday.

(*The Times, 2005*)

4. Scientific facts are presented as universal truths in the present tense.

Water <u>freezes</u> at 0 degrees.

Mammals <u>breastfeed</u> their young.

Go to www.routledge.com/cw/ross for Activity 8.3, Exploring the meanings conveyed by the present tense. **Y12+**

Application to standard English

Although pupils' use most verb structures without a problem, there is a significant variation between standard and non-standard English in the use of the auxiliary 'to do'. The use of a 'double negative' is considered non-standard in English grammar and thus inappropriate in formal contexts:

I did<u>n't</u> do <u>nothing</u>.

The explanation for this rule is often based on mathematics: two negatives make a positive. This rule, however, cannot be applied to language, as many languages use two negatives as the standard grammatical structure.

Je <u>ne</u> sais <u>pas</u>.

Although non-standard in English grammar, double negatives are used for emphasis, rather than to cancel each other out. It is important for pupils to recognise such structures as a non-standard, or dialectal, variation. They may occur in scripted dialogue to convey the speaker's social or educational background.

Go to www.routledge.com/cw/ross for Activity 8.4, Exploring the effect of non-standard forms. **Y8+**

Referring to the future

Other languages have a future tense: the form of the main verb changes by the addition of suffixes. Although there is no verb ending to indicate future time in English, there are various auxiliary verbs used to refer to the future.

 Go to www.routledge.com/cw/ross for Activity 8.5, Identifying different forms used to indicate future time in English. **Y11+**

Applications to language variation and change

The most common auxiliary used for future time is 'going to'. This expresses the speaker's intentions.

> *I'm going to travel by train.*

Non-native speakers tend to choose the simpler form 'will'.

> *I will travel by train.*

But this auxiliary verb is used by native speakers to express more certainty, often unrelated to the speaker's intentions:

> *The train will arrive at platform five.*

It is also possible to use the present simple or present continuous, if the context makes the future reference clear.
Present simple to express future time:

> *Today was the most terrible day of my life. My mother has got a job doing her rotten typing in an insurance office! She <u>starts</u> on Monday! Mr Lucas works at the same place. He is going to give her a lift every day.*
> (Sue Townsend, The Secret Diary of Adrian Mole aged 13¾)

Present continuous to express future time:

> *It's my mother's birthday on Saturday. I'<u>m organising</u> a surprise party.*

The conventions for using the auxiliary verbs 'will' v. 'shall' have changed in recent years. At one time, it was standard English to use 'shall' for first person and 'will' for second and third person:

> *I <u>shall</u> ask for a day off.*
> *You / he / she / they <u>will</u> ask for a day off.*

The use of 'shall' for second or third person was, thus, stylistically marked as emphatic:

> *Cinderella, you <u>shall</u> go to the ball.*
>
> *We <u>shall</u> overcome someday.*

However, in contemporary language use, 'shall' is comparatively rare. It has been replaced by 'will' in most cases. Although a search engine, such as Google, produces thousands of examples of 'shall', many are taken from crafted written language, such as song lyrics, poems or speeches. It tends to convey a more stylised effect, or suggest an older style of language.

Verb aspects

Glossary
aspect   continuous   perfect   perfect   continuous

This section will be brief, as explicit knowledge of verb **aspect** does not have many applications – to language use and style. Native English speakers instinctively use all these forms appropriately. However, teachers may like to be familiar with the terminology. It is used in TESOL – Teaching English to Speakers of Other Languages – and may be used in A-level language courses. These six aspects bring the number of verb phrase structures to eight:

	continuous	*perfect*	*perfect continuous*
present	*I am jumping*	*I have jumped*	*I have been jumping*
past	*I was jumping*	*I had jumped*	*I had been jumping*

These refer to various aspects of time: whether the action is ongoing or seen from a recent perspective.

Simple present/past

Do you drink beer? (ever)	*Are you drinking beer?* (at this moment)
I wrote my essay. (last night)	*I was writing my essay.* (all night)
She was in hospital. (last week)	*She has been in hospital.* (sometime)
My friend left the party. (at 11pm)	*My friend had left the party.* (before I arrived)

Rather than using a complex system of suffixes, as happens in Romance languages such as French, Italian or Spanish, English grammar uses more complex verb phrases. These two auxiliary verbs are inserted before the headword:

> *to be*
>
> *to have*

Continuous

The verb 'to be' is used to convey **continuous** – or ongoing – actions either in the present or past. The main verb takes the suffix –*ing*.

> *I am listening to radio.*   *I was waiting for hours.*

N.B. Some grammar books use the term 'progressive' rather than 'continuous'.

Perfect

The verb 'to have' is used to convey a recent perspective, either in the present or past. The main verb takes the suffix –*ed* (or irregular forms of the past participle).

> *The train has left.*   *I realised my watch had disappeared.*

The term for this aspect is **perfect**.

The two auxiliary verbs can be combined to form the present **perfect continuous** and the past perfect continuous. The main verb takes the suffix –*ing*.

> *I have been waiting for hours now.   She had been hoping he would phone.*

Verb moods

Glossary
mood   indicative   imperative   subjunctive   conditional   modal auxiliary verb

The eight verb phrase structures in previous examples were all in the **indicative** mood: expressing events actually happening over various periods of time. There are three other **moods** for verbs in English.

1   The term **imperative** refers to verbs expressing commands, instructions and requests.

> *Leave me alone. Don't ask me again.*

The form of the imperative is very simple in English: the base form of the verb without any suffixes or auxiliary verbs. The negative is formed with 'don't'.

2   The term **subjunctive** refers to hypothetical situations, such as 'If I ruled the world…'

In languages such as French and Italian, there are separate subjunctive tenses with complex verb endings. In contemporary English there is little evidence of verb forms that mark out a subjunctive mood, but some set phrases remain, using forms of the verb 'to be'.

subjunctive	*indicative*
if I <u>were</u> you	*if I was you*
as it <u>were</u>	*as it is/was*
so <u>be</u> it	*so it is*
<u>be</u> that as it may	*that is as it is*

Other verbs in English 'borrow' the past tense form to indicate that a situation is hypothetical, rather than a definite possibility.

hypothetical	*definite possibility*
If I <u>ruled</u> the world	*If I rule the world*

3   The term **conditional** is often used to label forms of verbs that indicate events that are possible under certain conditions.

When speculating, or hypothesising, pupils will intuitively change the form of the verb from its usual indicative, by inserting other auxiliary verbs. They can demonstrate this in response to questions introduced by 'if' or 'suppose'.

 Go to www.routledge.com/cw/ross for Activity 8.6, Showing the use of auxiliary verbs for speculating or hypothesising. **Y8+**

Modal auxiliary verbs

Apart from the three primary auxiliary verbs mentioned earlier, there is another group of auxiliary verbs. This group of **modal auxiliary verbs** have significant effects on meaning. They are used to convey various notions such as possibility, probability, necessity or obligation.

can	*could*
will	*would*
shall	*should*
may	*might*
must	*ought to*

Form and functions

These ten modal auxiliary verbs never change in form. No suffixes are added for third person (*'she cans'), or for changes to aspect (*I am maying; *we have musted'). The grouping in pairs above shows that the second form can sometimes be used as the past tense.

There are a few other verbs that function as modal auxiliaries, expressing similar meanings. Their form, however, is slightly different. These verbs do change form, adding the suffixes –*s*, –*ing* and –*ed*.

have to	*she has to/is having to/had to*
need to	*he needs to/was needing to/needed to*

Modal verbs express a variety of meanings, with subtle shades of meaning and some overlap. This makes their use in texts significant and worth close examination.

Possibility–probability

Some modal verbs indicate the degree of possibility of an event. Some of the verbs were listed in pairs above, with the second form sometimes used as the past tense. For example:

I can ride a bike.	*I could ride a bike when I was five years old.*
I will be famous one day.	*I always thought I would be famous.*
We shall be free.	*I believed we should be free.*
I may go to university.	*My parents hoped I might go to university.*

Apart from expressing either present or past time, these verbs express the attitude of the speaker to the degree of possibility of that event happening.

I will be famous.

I could be famous.

I may be famous.

I might be famous.

One use of the modal verb 'must' is to convey this type of conjecture:

She must have left.   (*I suppose she has left.*)

When reading texts, pupils should be able to identify the use of modal verbs and explain the attitudes implied. This is particularly useful in analysis of persuasive texts.

 Go to www.routledge.com/cw/ross for Activity 8.7, Analysing the use of modal verbs in a speech by Martin Luther King. **Y10+**

Politeness and formality

These modal auxiliary verbs also function to indicate degrees of politeness and formality. For example:

Can you lend me five pounds?	(*direct, colloquial*)
Will you lend me five pounds?	(*direct*)
Could you lend me five pounds?	(*tentative, more polite and formal*)

Would you lend me five pounds?   (*tentative, more polite and formal*)

May I borrow five pounds?   (*more formal and polite*)

Might I borrow five pounds?   (*tentative, polite and formal*)

Necessity–obligation

As well as indicating degrees of possibility and politeness, some modal auxiliary verbs express degrees of necessity or obligation. The writer or speaker can convey their attitude in ways that range from tentative suggestions to firm instructions. For example:

You *might* try alternative therapies.   (*tentative suggestion*)

You *should* try alternative therapies.   (*advice*)

You *ought* to try alternative therapies.   (*firmer advice*)

You *need* to try alternative therapies.   (*definite suggestion*)

You *have* to try alternative therapies.   (*definite instruction*)

You *must* try alternative therapies.   (*perhaps even more direct?*)

It is important to recognise the use of modal verbs and phrases, as their function is to convey the speaker's – or writer's – attitude to the event referred to by the main verb. These auxiliary verbs allow speakers and writers to speculate and hypothesise, as well as to relate actual events. There are also modal phrases, which indicate degrees of possibility and certainty:

perhaps, maybe, surely, I suppose/think/guess

 Go to www.routledge.com/cw/ross for Activity 8.8, Analysing the use and effect of modal auxiliary verbs in narrative fiction. **Y11+**

Implied meanings

The modal auxiliary verb 'would' can convey different meanings. It can be used in a straightforward way to convey past events, with the added suggestion that they are regular actions. This provides a way for pupils to vary their use of tenses in writing about the past.

This extract from a novel uses 'would' to convey a sense of exasperation that these events happened without fail:

The white miner <u>would pretend</u> to give the orders, but it knew that it <u>would be</u> the boss boy who really got the work done. But a stupid white miner – and there were plenty of those – <u>would drive</u> his team too hard. He <u>would shout</u> and hit the men if he thought they were not working quickly enough and this could be very dangerous.

(Alexander McCall Smith, The Ladies No. 1 Detective Agency)

This is an indicative use of the auxiliary verb, but the same verb 'would' can also be used to express hypothetical situations. In persuasive texts, the writer may slip from one use to another, disguising the fact that some comments are simply the writer's speculation.

In the extract in Activity 8.9, the detective writer Patricia Cornwell is giving her theory about the identity of Jack the Ripper. She begins with modal verbs and phrases, clearly indicating that this is conjecture, but moves into more definite statements, implying that certain events actually took place.

 Go to www.routledge.com/cw/ross for Activity 8.9, Analysing the meanings implied by different verb moods. **Y12+**

Verb voice

'The whereabouts of Osama bin Laden is unknown.'

So what assumptions are in the sentence 'The whereabouts of Osama bin Laden is unknown'? It assumes that at the moment anyone is reading the sentence, they do not know where bin Laden is. That's anyone alive in the world. The words 'unknown' and 'not known' have the sense of 'not known to any human anywhere', as in, say, 'there is no known cure for malaria'. Clearly, this didn't apply to bin Laden. Presumably, he knew where he was, along with a group of his followers.

So why do many of us reading a sentence like that without instantly finding it odd or illogical? It was published in western newspapers in the context of what western security forces were intending to do in Afghanistan. No sentence stands entirely on its own. It is, if you like, always coloured by what's being said or written around it. So, hidden in the sentence is a sense that was what being spoken about, was a western point of view, i.e. 'bin Laden's whereabouts is unknown to the West.'

(Rosen, The Power of the Passive, *2002*)

The final way of classifying verb phrases is by their **voice**. The distinction between the active and passive voice requires some explicit teaching. The form of the passive is quite complex and acquired relatively late by children. Pupils should be able to use the passive voice in formal, impersonal situations.

But the use of the passive is significant in other ways. The above extract from an article (Rosen, 2002) provides some interesting points about the assumptions that may be embedded in the use of the passive.

Changes from active to passive

It is sometimes assumed that the passive is simply a more formal version of an active sentence, but conveying the same meaning:

> *A dog bit my brother.*   *(active voice)*
>
> *My brother was bitten by a dog.*   *(passive voice)*

The point of view or emphasis has changed. The norm is for verbs to be used in the **active voice**, emphasising the role of the 'agent' – the dog.

Such structures can be transformed into the **passive voice**, which places emphasis on the recipient of the action – the brother. The agent can be mentioned, as above, or omitted:

> *My brother was bitten.*

Some passive constructions are common in everyday language:

> *I was born in Cairo.*

It is interesting that the active version is never used to emphasise the agent – the mother – and the action:

> *? My mother bore me.*

Active structures, such as 'Mary begat Jesus', only occur in older texts.

Form

Non-native users of English find the structure of passive verb phrases tricky to learn. Activities such as the following will demonstrate pupils' intuitive ability to use passive constructions.

 Go to www.routledge.com/cw/ross for Activity 8.10, Changing sentences from active to passive voice. **Y7+**

Tests

 Go to www.routledge.com/cw/ross for Activity 8.11, Using tests of insertion and deletion to show the structure of passive verb phrases. **Y8+**

Functions of passive verbs

The passive voice places emphasis is on the action itself, or the recipient of the action, rather than the agent. Although it is commonly assumed that the passive voice is simply a marker of formality, this change of focus happens for various reasons and therefore has slightly different effects. Some of the functions of the passive are listed below with examples.

1   It is used in scientific reports where the identity of the agent is not important:

   The crystals <u>were heated</u> over a bunsen burner and sulphuric acid was added.

2   It is used in news reports where the identity of the agent is unknown:

   Two million pounds <u>were stolen</u> in a post office robbery.

3   However, it may also be used to avoid identifying the agent:

   Six blacks <u>were shot</u> in Soweto. (by the police)

4   Or to leave the claim unsubstantiated:

   Archer <u>was regarded</u> as a hero.

5   It is often used in academic genres and tends to convey a more detached tone:

   It <u>was felt</u> that Wolsey had grown too powerful.

6   However, this may also be considered a way of avoiding mention of the agent – the authority for the statement remains vague, and may simply be the opinion of the writer:

   Jane Austen's style <u>is said</u> to be flowery.

 Go to www.routledge.com/cw/ross for Activity 8.12, Identifying the use and effect of the passive voice. **Y10+**

Compound verb phrases

The previous examples in this section showed the various possible structures for a *single* main verb. There is one further structure of verb phrases. It is very common and used intuitively.

Some verbs can combine with other main verbs to form a longer phrase. Some common examples are verbs expressing desires and intentions:

want	*I want to go/see/meet*
hope	*I hope to pass/succeed/save*
need	*I need to pay/leave/*

love	*I love to cook / read / run*
like	*I like to dance / write / travel*
stop	*I stop to listen / look / stare*

These all use the infinitive form – to + verb – to combine the two main verbs. Some verbs are combined using the present participle:

enjoy	*I enjoy dancing / reading / studying*

Some verbs can use either structure:

like	*I like to travel. I like travelling.*

In some cases, this changes the meaning:

stop	*I stopped to listen. I stopped listening.*

These types of verbs can be combined into a longer string:

I expected to be able to enjoy relaxing.

Verb phrase summary

In English, verb phrases take different forms to indicate various functions and meanings.

TABLE 8.1 Verb phrases summary

Form	The main verb can take suffixes '–s', '–ing', '–ed'. Primary auxiliary verbs can be used before the main verb: 'do', 'be', 'have'. Modal auxiliaries can also come before the main verb.
Functions	The verb phrase can express mood, voice, tense and aspect:

mood	indicative	imperative	subjunctive	conditional
voice	active	passive		
tense	present	past		
aspect	continuous	perfect	continuous perfect	

Meanings	verb phrases convey subtle shades of meaning, relating to: time duration perspective degrees of possibility, necessity, obligation, politeness, formality

CHAPTER

Clauses

This chapter moves up to the next level of grammar – the way phrases combine to form clauses.

TABLE 9.1 Levels of structure

One or more **morphemes**	combine to form	words.
One or more **words**	combine to form	phrases.
One or more **phrases**	combine to form	clauses.
One or more **clauses**	combine to form	sentences.
One or more **sentences**	combine to form	paragraphs and whole texts.

The five different types of phrase can be printed on individual cards. This allows pupils to experiment with the familiar tests of substitution, deletion, insertion and transposition in a physical way. The activities, which only take a few hours of group work, consolidate their understanding of phrase structure and demonstrate the seven types of clause.

This chapter on clause structure deals with *main* clauses. A main clause can stand alone, so, in this sense, this chapter explores the structure of simple sentences. This level of grammar provides the basis for study of more complex sentence structures in Chapter 10, which distinguishes between main and *subordinate* clauses.

A few key terms, such as 'subject', 'verb' and 'adverbial', are introduced to describe the roles of phrases within clauses. (Capital letters are used to distinguish between the term 'verb' or 'adverb' to describe a word class, and the use of a similar term to describe the function of a phrase in clause structure.)

This explicit knowledge is applied to the study of poetry, showing how the usual structures may be rearranged for stylistic effect. It is also used to reinforce pupils' awareness of punctuation conventions, in particular the use of full stops between main clauses.

What is a clause?

simple sentence   clause   main v. subordinate   finite v non-finite verb

---

I pull my hand away from her kitten, slowly. I step back.

I can't leave.

I'm losing the light. The shed gets darker. Shadows play tricks on my eyes. I manoeuvre the carrier into the drywall.

I send her a telepathic thought. Please just go forward, and it will be all right. I sit in that shed a long time.

She goes forward. I close the carrier door and she is finally, mercifully trapped.

I take down the barricade. I triumphantly hand the box with the kittens to the neighbourhood caretaker. I am shattered. And I am humbled.

I say a silent prayer, a plea for forgiveness, to this little one, the one that I missed.

(Extracts taken from Satsuma *by Elizabeth Cava*, www.faunaoutreach.org/satsuma*)*

Clauses and sentences

It is rare to find texts that use mostly simple, one-clause sentences. Even stories for young children – and writing by young children – include longer sentences, combining more than one clause. However, the use of such simple structures can have some dramatic impact, as the above account of a cat-rescue organisation shows.

The writer uses many **simple sentences.** This grammatical term needs some clarification. 'Simple' does not mean that the sentence is short, as the following examples show:

> *Please just go forward, and it will be all right.*
>
> *I triumphantly hand the box with the kittens to the neighbourhood caretaker.*

The longer second example is a simple sentence, as it contains one clause. The first shorter sentence combines two clauses with the conjunction 'and'. This leaves the question: What is a **clause**? The essential element of a clause is the verb – each clause contains one verb phrase. If pupils can identify the verbs in the sentences above, they will see that the first sentence has two verb phrases: 'go' and 'will be', forming two separate clauses. The second sentence has only one verb: 'hand', so there is one clause.

A **main clause** is one that can stand alone. This explanation relies on an intuitive sense of grammatical structure. For example, the difference between:

> *Shadows play tricks on my eyes.*
>
> ** Shadows playing tricks on my eyes…*

The second sentence does not make complete sense. It suggests that something further is going to be added.

A more explicit definition of a main clause involves the concepts of finite v. non-finite verbs. This is explored in more detail in Chapter 10. **Finite verb** forms can stand alone, making complete grammatical sense.

> *I _pull_ my hand away from her kitten. I _step_ back.*

Chapter 10 looks at subordinate clauses in more detail, but a brief explanation of the distinction between 'finite' and 'non-finite' verbs, and 'main' and 'subordinate' clauses, is included here.

Non-finite verb forms are the present and past participles, ending in *–ing* or *–ed*. They do not make complete grammatical sense.

> *<u>Pulling</u> my hand away from her kitten…*

Non-finite verbs can be used as connectives, linking a **subordinate clause** to a following main clause.

> **<u>Pulling</u> my hand away from her kitten, I step back.*

The next section shows how phrases are combined to form various structures of clauses.

The seven patterns of clause structure

Glossary
subject verb   transitive v. intransitive   object   direct v. indirect object   complement   adverbial

There are seven basic clause structures in English. Six of these patterns are used in the short extract above.

1. *I can't leave.*
2. *I step back.*
3. *I'm losing the light.*
4. *The shed gets darker.*
5. *I send her a telepathic thought.*
6. *Shadows play tricks on my eyes.*

A rephrasing of the sixth provides an example of the seventh:

7. *The shadows make me confused.*

The following activities explore these seven clause structures, using the tests of substitution, insertion, deletion and transposition. The elements of structure can best be demonstrated by activities that allow pupils to physically move the key elements around.

Twenty-four cards should be made from the following phrases. (The choice of phrases is inspired by the bizarre cartoons of Gary Larson, in order to capture the imagination of pupils.) The activities can be made slightly easier by colour-coding each type of phrase.

Widow Twankey	*another alligator shoe*
an ageing beetle	*that band of head-hunters*
the politician	*one stale meat pasty*
irresistible	*most peculiar indeed*
dozed	*leapt*
tripped up	*should have placed*
wanted to hide	*was*
had abandoned	*skinned*
sent	*found*
with a broken spear	*on the porch*
in the hollow tree	*out of the blue*
before breakfast	*morosely*

Types of phrase

 Go to www.routledge.com/cw/ross for Activity 9.1, Grouping the cards into the five different types of phrase. **Y9+**

Combining phrases

N.B. Do not use *two* verb phrases for the following activities.

For example, do not combine 'was' with another verb like 'tripped up', as this makes a single passive verb phrase. Also do not combine 'found' with another verb like 'skinned' as this will make a complex sentence with a subordinate clause, introduced by a verb with the suffix *-ed*:

The politician <u>found</u> an ageing beetle <u>skinned</u> on the porch.

 Go to www.routledge.com/cw/ross for Activity 9.2, Using intuitive understanding to create clauses from phrases. **Y9+**

Clause type 1

 Go to www.routledge.com/cw/ross for Activity 9.3, Creating the most simple clause structure: subject + verb. **Y9+**

Applications to style

Pupils should recognise when it is effective to use short, direct sentences. This simple subject + verb (sv) structure of a clause conveys the minimum information: the agent and the action. The clause can be formed from two words, or a more complex noun phrase and verb phrase:

Subject	*Verb*
Era	*ends.*
An era	*has ended.*
The Mode Daily Sweepstakes	*has ended.*
Email service from libraryreference.com	*is going to end.*

This structure tends to be used for dramatic impact, making a brief assertion that is later developed or explained.

The woman/wept.

No-one/spoke.

Research into pupils' writing at GCSE shows that the occasional use of such simple sentences is a feature of A-grade performance. Lower grades tend to lack this confident variety of sentence structures, using a sequence of longer sentences.

Transitive v. intransitive verbs

This simple clause structure with a subject and verb is only possible with **intransitive** verbs. This term is used for verbs that can stand alone. Transitive verbs, in contrast, require another element to make complete sense. The following **transitive** verbs cannot be used in this simple structure: *was*, *had abandoned*, *should have placed*, *skinned*, *sent*, *found*.

* *The politician sent...*

Some verbs can be used in either a transitive or intransitive sense: 'tripped up', 'wanted to hide'

The politician wanted to hide an ageing beetle.	*(transitive)*
The politician wanted to hide.	*(intransitive)*

This distinction is understood intuitively, so does not need to be explained for pupils' own language use. It can, however, be used to comment on the ways meanings may be implied in texts.

For example, in popular romantic fiction, the female character tends to be associated with intransitive verbs – 'she breathed/smiled/sighed', etc – whereas transitive verbs occur more often with the male character's actions – 'he kissed her/took her in his arms'. This may suggest that the male character has more impact on the world around him.

The linguist Norman Fairclough notes the choice of intransitive verbs in government statements, such as 'Weak teachers will go'. Rather than expressing this as an action on the part of the authorities – 'We will sack weak teachers' – the choice of an intransitive verb suggests that these teachers will simply disappear of their own accord!

Clause type 2

 Go to www.routledge.com/cw/ross for Activity 9.4, Building on the basic structure of Subject + Verb, by inserting a third element – an Adverbial. **Y9+**.

Application to style

This SVA (subject + verb + adverbial) structure of clauses is very common. It occurs in all types of language use. (The previous sentence uses this structure.) The noun phrase and adverbial phrase can be expanded into more complex structures, but the basic clause structure remains simple. The following examples are taken from poetry and academic writing.

S	V	A
He	*collapses*	*like a balloon*
Dragon-lovers with sweet serious eyes	*brood*	*in a desert wood thick with bluebells*
		(Ted Hughes, 'Moon-Whales')
The long light	*shakes*	*across the lakes, (and)*
the wild cataract	*leaps*	*in glory.*
The splendour	*falls*	*on castle walls*
		(Tennyson, 'The Princess')

This basic SVA structure can be varied for stylistic effect. Pupils should be aware that the position of the adverbial phrase is flexible. In imaginative forms of writing, such as poetry, the adverbial may be placed at the beginning of the structure for emphasis, or rhythmic effect.

A	S	V
Full fathom five	*thy father*	*lies*
		(Shakespeare, The Tempest)

Under a pool of streetlights	*the boy*	*stops.*

(Hathorn and Rogers, 1994)

Occasionally, the order of subject and verb can be changed:

A	*V*	*S*
In every moon-mirror	*lurks*	*a danger.*

This basic structure is also found in formal, academic writing:

S	*V*	*A*
A wide variety of animals	*deceive*	*intermittently.*

The simple sentence may seem more complex, if the adverbial phrase is expanded for more precise detail:

S	*V*	*A*
A few unfortunates	*suffer*	*from a puzzling deficit, an inability to understand another's point of view.*

(Aitchison, 1996)

Clause type 3

There are other types of clause structure that use three phrases.

 Go to www.routledge.com/cw/ross for Activity 9.5, Creating three-part clauses from subject + (transitive) verb + object. **Y9+**

Application to style

This is the most simple clause structure using transitive verbs: a subject followed by a verb and an object. Each of the phrases can be a single word, or expanded into more complex phrases.

S	*V*	*O*
I	*'ve known*	*rivers.*
I	*'ve known*	*rivers ancient as the world and older than the flow of human blood in human veins.*

(Langston Hughes, 'The Negro Speaks of Rivers')

Poetry provides examples of unusual clause structures, even reversing subject and object, for emphasis or rhythmic effect:

O	*A*	*A*	*S*	*V*
a damsel with a dulcimer	*in a vision*	*once*	*I*	*saw.*

(Coleridge, 'Xanadu Khubla Khan')

Formal, academic writing also uses this basic clause structure in simple sentences:

S	V	O
True deceit	*involves*	*'tactical deception'.*

But the use of simple sentences often seems more complex, because the noun phrases are expanded:

> *Possibly only one primate branch, the great apes, /has/a true theory of mind, the ability to attribute intentions to others.*

> *(Aitchison, 1996)*

Clause type 4

There is another clause structure using three elements. The verb 'to be' is the most commonly used verb, but operates in different ways. Its function is 'stative', rather than 'dynamic', as it expresses a state or condition. Other verbs that share this function are: 'appear', 'seem', 'look', 'sound', etc.

 Go to www.routledge.com/cw/ross for Activity 9.6, Creating 3-part clause structures with Subject + (stative/copular) Verb + Complement. **Y9+**

Application to style

The SVC structure is common in all types of language use. The following examples are taken from poems and academic writing.

S	V	C
some people	*are*	*flower lovers.*
I	*'m*	*a weed lover. (Nicholson, 'Weeds')*
The gesture theory	*is*	*an old one. (Aitchison, 1996)*

The noun and adjectival phrases may be simple, or expanded into more complex phrases:

> *Nasturtiums on earth/are/small and seething with horrible green caterpillars.*
> *(Ted Hughes, 'Moon-Whales')*

> *This property of displacement/is/one of language's most valuable characteristics.*
> *(Aitchison, 1996)*

Although it is grammatically possible to transpose the subject, verb and complement, this stylistic variation tends to occur in imaginative writing. The unusual word order places emphasis on the quality of the subject.

C	*V*	*S*	
All mimsy	*were*	*the borrogroves.*	(Carroll, 'The Jabberwocky')
Marvellously white	*is*	*the moon-lily.*	(Hughes, 'Moon-Whales')

The adjectival phrase can be expanded:

> *Broad, soft, silent and white and like a huge barn-owl's/is/their flight.*
>
> (Hughes, 'Moon-Whales')

The Subject can also be expanded by adding an extra phrase at the end:

> *Such a peculiar lot/we/are, we people without money.*
>
> (James Berry, 'Fantasy of an African Boy')

Clause type 5

So far, we have seen three possible clause structures with three elements: the obligatory Subject and Verb may be followed by an adverbial, an object or a complement.

 Go to www.routledge.com/cw/ross for Activity 9.7, Creating four-part clause structures using object + complement after certain types of verb. **Y10+**

Application to style

This structure is comparatively rare in language use, as it occurs with a limited number of verbs. Even when such verbs are used, writers often prefer to make the structure explicit by inserting the verb 'to be':

> *The market manager thought it [was] a serious matter.*

Clause type 6

 Go to www.routledge.com/cw/ross for Activity 9.8, Creating four-part clause structures with direct and indirect objects after certain types of verb. **Y10+**

Application to style

In languages such as German, there is a separate 'case' (noun suffix) for direct v. indirect objects. As there are no such suffixes to indicate the role of nouns in English, the indirect object is often made more explicit by rephrasing the sentence. For example:

> *The manager wrote Mr Hook a letter.*
> *That very day the market manager wrote a letter to Mr Hook.*

Clause type 7

The previous six structures form the basis of most clauses in English grammar. However, there are a few verbs that require an adverbial after the Object.

S	V	O	A
I	*pull*	*my hand*	*away.*
Shadows	*play*	*tricks*	*on my eyes.*
She	*left*	*her money*	*beside the chair.*

Go to www.routledge.com/cw/ross for Activity 9.9, Creating four-part clause structures using an object and adverbial after certain types of verb. **Y11+**

Expanding basic clause structures

Apart from a few verbs, Adverbial phrases are generally optional extras, providing more information about the time, place or manner of the event. Preposition and adverbial phrases are very flexible, allowing many variations to the basic structure of clauses:

- More than one adverbial phrase can be inserted.
- Adverbial phrases can be placed in various positions in the structure.

In the first activity, pupils expanded the clause by adding as many adverbials as possible.

Go to www.routledge.com/cw/ross for Activity 9.10, Expanding clause structures by inserting optional elements – adverbials. **Y7+**

Application to style

The following examples are taken from the account of a cat-rescue operation provided at the beginning of the chapter. They show the flexibility possible in the use of adverbial phrases.

Adverbial phrases are commonly placed at the end of clauses, providing more detail about the event: how, when and where?

I/pull/my hand/<u>away from her kitten,</u>/<u>slowly</u>.

It is possible to use three adverbials, without 'cluttering' the structure of the clause.

She gazes/<u>down at us</u>/<u>serenely</u>/<u>from her safe haven</u>.

Stylistic variation is possible with the position of adverbials. Single words are commonly transposed to the beginning of the structure for emphasis:

> _Slowly_ I pull my hand away from the kitten.
>
> _Serenely_ she gazes down at us from her safe haven.

It is less common to place a phrase at the beginning of the structure, but it can be done for emphasis. In this case, a comma is normally used to separate the phrase from the subject:

> _From her safe haven_, she gazes down at us serenely.

Adverbials – generally single words – can also be placed before or after the verb.

> I _triumphantly_ hand the box with the kittens to the neighbourhood caretaker.
>
> It is _always_ the one I missed.

 Go to www.routledge.com/cw/ross for Activity 9.11, Analysing the position and effect of adverbial phrases in poetry. **Y10+**

Applications to punctuation

A common error in punctuation is the use of a 'comma-splice' rather than a full stop. This usually happens when pupils use short, one-clause sentences. It may be because they associate the use of full stops with pauses for breath. It is more reliable to see punctuation as marking grammatical divisions. Thus, the full stop divides complete clauses – simple sentences. The easiest way to recognise a clause is to identify verbs as they are the essential element of any clause.

The following example of a 'comma-splice' shows two verbs in two separate clauses.

> I _started to peer_ around the garden, I _noticed_ Jim Boulder's car outside their garage.

Commas may be used before connectives to separate a subordinate clause, or to separate phrases within the clause:

> The robbers aren't going to come through the entrance, _so_ they would go through the back.
>
> _Behind the hedge_, I thought I saw a movement.

 Go to www.routledge.com/cw/ross for Activity 9.12, Using knowledge of clause structure to understand where full stops are needed instead of commas. **Y7+**

Applications to style

Pupils may be reluctant to signal their use of simple, one-clause sentences with a clear full stop if they believe that good writing is characterised by long, complex sentences. They should notice how effective short sentences can be by looking at examples such as the following.

George Orwell's prose style is a good example of his principles for writing. He believed that 'the great enemy of clear language is insincerity'. His style is strong and economical, using a number of effective short simple sentences. He also uses simple co-ordinating conjunctions: 'but' and 'and'.

 Go to www.routledge.com/cw/ross for Activity 9.13, Analysing the use and effect of simple sentences in George Orwell's *Shooting an Elephant*. **Y10+**

Summary clause structure

There are seven basic clause structures in English:

- Subject + Verb
- Subject + Verb + Adverbial
- Subject + Verb + Object
- Subject + Verb + Complement
- Subject + Verb + Object + Complement
- Subject + Verb + indirect Object + direct Object
- Subject + Verb + Object + Adverbial

Clauses are formed by combining phrases. The essential element of any clause is the Verb. This chapter looked at main clauses – or simple sentences – which also have a noun phrase as subject. Other clause structures are formed by adding phrases as an object, complement, or adverbial.

I/can't leave.	$S + V$
I/step/back.	$S + V + A$
I'm losing/the light.	$S + V + O$
The shed/gets/darker.	$S + V + C$
The shadows/make/me/confused.	$S + V + O + C$
I/send/her/a telepathic thought.	$S + V + Oi + Od$
Shadows/play/tricks/on my eyes.	$S + V + O + A$

The usual order in English grammar is to begin with the subject and verb, but this pattern can be varied for stylistic effect. The most flexible element of clause structure is the adverbial – either an adverbial or prepositional phrase. These are normally optional elements; more than one can be added in a variety of positions in the structure.

The next chapter looks at the ways clauses are combined to form a variety of sentence structures.

10

Sentences

This chapter moves to the highest level of grammar – the structure of sentences from clauses.

TABLE 10.1 Levels of structure

One or more **morphemes**	combine to form	words.
One or more **words**	combine to form	phrases.
One or more **phrases**	combine to form	clauses.
One or more **clauses**	combine to form	sentences.
One or more **sentences**	combine to form	paragraphs and whole texts.

This is as far as the study of grammar, or syntax, can take us. The organisation of paragraphs and the structure of different genres of texts is examined in Chapters 13 and 14.

Sentences can be classified in two ways: according to their *function* – to make statements, ask questions, give commands – as well as their *structure* – simple, compound or complex. This chapter builds on the awareness of simple sentences formed from one clause, introduced in the previous chapter. The familiar tests of insertion and deletion tests demonstrate ways in which compound and complex sentences are formed. Different types of connective are introduced, explaining the key terms: conjunctions, non-finite verbs and subordinate clauses. The test of deletion is used to clarify the difference between main and subordinate clause and explain the use of commas within sentences. The transposition test is used to demonstrate the ways that subordinate clauses can be moved for emphasis.

This technical understanding is applied to use of appropriate styles in writing. The effects on style of using various types and combinations of sentence structure are explored, using examples of writing for different purposes and audiences.

Functions of Sentences

This section introduces one useful way of classifying sentences – by their function. The informal terms – statement, question, command – can be used, but the technical terms are introduced for more precision.

declarative   interrogative   imperative   exclamatory

Wouldn't it be great to...

Learn the Magic Words and Phrases to gain the Advantage in any Verbal Encounter!

Have you ever noticed that it's the best talkers, the ones able to win in a verbal wrestling match that gain the success, the promotions, the extra sales, the popularity and the position of authority we would all like?

> *Now…never again find yourself at a loss for words*

> *Now…never again come off second best in any verbal encounter*

> *Now…never again wish that you had spoken up, made your point more strongly or stopped someone else's bad behaviour*

In this special report you will meet one of the world's leading authorities on personal communication and discover the secrets of CONVERSATION POWER. Plus you are invited to try his methods FREE FOR 30 DAYS.

(advertising leaflet, prepared by Vic Conant, President of Nightingale Conant)

The text above uses three different functions of sentences to achieve its persuasive purpose. It addresses the reader directly by asking questions at the beginning, before suggesting actions and then providing information in statements. It does not actually use the fourth function – an exclamatory sentence – but an exclamation mark follows one of the questions. These four functions of sentences will be explained, using the accepted terminology for the different structures.

Making statements

The norm for writing is **declarative** sentences, often used to make statements. In this structure, the subject comes before the verb (underlined).

> *In this special report <u>you will meet</u> one of the world's leading authorities…*
>
> *Plus <u>you are invited to try</u> his methods.*

Asking questions

In English grammar, **interrogatives** are formed by moving the verb before the subject. This is straightforward for most verb phrases. If there is an auxiliary verb, this is moved before the subject.

> <u>*Wouldn't it*</u> *be great … to Learn the Magic Words… !*

Have you ever noticed … ?

Interrogatives are easily recognised by the use of question marks – even though the first example actually uses an exclamation mark.

N.B. As Chapter 9 showed, the auxiliary verb *to do* is used to form questions in the present and past tense. As it has no other function in such structures, it is sometimes called the 'dummy do'.

Do you like shopping?

Did you always enjoy shopping?

Giving instructions

Imperative sentences, used to express instructions, commands or suggestions, use the simple form of the infinitive, often with the verb 'to do' for negatives.

Go to the shops.

Don't take the bus.

The advertising leaflet above uses imperatives such as:

Find yourself at a loss for words

The negative word 'never' is used instead of 'don't':

Never come off second best in any verbal encounter

Often instructions are 'softened' by the use of modal verbs such as 'must', 'ought to', or 'should':

You should go to the shops.

You mustn't take the bus.

Making exclamations

Exclamatory structures are comparatively rare in spoken and written English, although the exclamation mark is often used to emphasise statements. Strictly speaking, exclamatory sentences are formed by the use of 'how' or 'what'. They differ from interrogatives, as the subject followed by verb order remains.

How I love shopping!

What a pleasure it is!

Pupils should be aware that exclamation marks are often over-used, conveying a very personal, excitable tone that it rarely appropriate in writing. The use of multiple exclamation marks should be reserved for communication between friends.

Applications to style

Pupils should be able to use a variety of sentence types in their writing for effects such as pace or emphasis. The use of interrogatives and imperatives in texts conveys a sense of personal interaction between writer and reader, or speaker and listener. Although this is not appropriate for texts such as essays, with an impersonal tone, addressing the reader directly can be effective in persuasive or instructional writing. Even in such texts, it is important to use these colloquial features with control.

 Go to www.routledge.com/cw/ross for Activity 10.1, Identifying sentence types and their effects in a pupil's writing to persuade. **Y10+**

Sentence structures

The other way of classifying types of sentences is by the complexity of their structure – simple, compound or complex. This distinction is useful for teachers, as these terms are used in mark-schemes to distinguish between levels of achievement. For example, pupils who use mainly simple and compound sentences, are assessed at a lower level. Those who use some complex sentences with conjunctions such as *because* achieve a slightly higher level. The use of a variety of sentence structures, including 'embedded' clauses and 'fronted' clauses for emphasis, is a marker of higher achievement.

Glossary
simple sentence   main verb

In summertime village cricket is a delight to everyone. Nearly every village has its own cricket field where the young men play and the old men watch. In the village of Lintz in the County of Durham they have their own ground, where they have played these last 70 years. They tend it well. The wicket area is well rolled and mown. The outfield is kept short. It has a good clubhouse for the players and seats for the onlookers. The village team plays there on Saturdays and Sundays. They belong to a league, competing with the neighbouring villages. On other evenings they practice while the light lasts. Yet now after these 70 years a judge of the High Court has ordered that they must not play anymore. He has issued an injunction to stop them. He has done it at the insistence of a newcomer who is no lover of cricket.

(Lord Denning, Law Report, Miller v. Jackson, 1977)

Use of simple sentences

The High Court judge, Lord Denning, was noted for his clarity of expression in legal reports – a genre usually characterised by its complex style. The extract above uses everyday vocabulary in a number of simple sentence structures.

A **simple sentence** consists of a single clause, i.e. containing one main verb.

> *In summertime village cricket is a delight to everyone.*
>
> *They tend it well.*
>
> *The wicket area is well rolled and mown.*
>
> *The outfield is kept short.*
>
> *It has a good clubhouse for the players and seats for the onlookers.*
>
> *The village team plays there on Saturdays and Sundays.*
>
> *He has issued an injunction to stop them.*

A simple sentence is not necessarily a short sentence, as the above examples show. However, the following activity shows the use of sentences that are clearly 'simple' – a single main clause formed from relatively short phrases. This is a feature of texts that require simplicity above all, for example, when writing for an audience of young children.

 Go to www.routledge.com/cw/ross for Activity 10.2, Identifying the use of simple sentences in writing for children (aged between five and eight years). **Y9+**

Application to style

Simple sentence structures can be effective in writing for certain audiences and purposes. There is a trend these days towards clarity in language use in public documents, with the Plain English campaign promoting more simplicity in style in their advice documents and annual awards. The previous chapters provided examples of writers, such as George Orwell and Ernest Hemingway, known for their use of an effectively simple style.

Although it is worth showing pupils how effective short, direct sentences can be, their position is significantly different from such established writers. The issue of competence and style in language use can be illustrated by the joke:

> *What is the definition of good taste?*
>
> *Someone who knows how to play the accordion, but chooses not to.*

The reader can assume that experienced writers have a full repertoire of language strategies and have made an informed decision – they know how to use complex sentences, but have chosen not to. Pupils, on the other hand, are at the stage of developing their language skills, so should display their competence in using a range of sentence structures. Most language use combines two or more clauses into longer sentences. This can be done in two ways: by *linking* main clauses into a compound sentence, or by *embedding* one, or more, subordinate clauses within a complex sentence.

Compound sentences

The first way of creating longer sentence structures is relatively simple, and acquired by children at an early stage of language development. Two or more clauses are linked in a simple sequence. The over-use of this style of sentence is a common weakness in pupils' writing – more so than the use of simple sentences. An explicit awareness of the structure of compound sentences may help when revising their work.

Glossary			
compound sentence	co-ordinating conjunction	main clause	finite v. non-finite verb

---

Becky came round to ours last week, but I don't think she's going to be good enough to get into the lacrosse team, because she's just on her computer all the time and she had the same trousers on that Marie's got, but they didn't look as good and anyway Marie got hers first. Marie keeps saying that she's a vegetarian, but I'm sure I saw a Pepperami sticking out of her bag. Anyway my Dad says that vegetarians are stupid, because all they do is eat chips and cheese and then they have a heart attack. David's having a party but it's going to be really bad, because his Mum's going to make the food and everyone had food poisoning last time and I don't care anyway, because I'm going to be in Spain. David's going to Barcelona, but he's only going for 10 days and we're going for two weeks and I've got my own room with a TV and everything.

(Neil Gaukwin, comedian and poet)

The example above is a parody of a young person's style of writing. The writer intuitively used long, mainly compound sentence structures to create a tone of excitable rambling, as one idea leads on to the next. The links between ideas are confined to simple addition – 'and' – or opposition – 'but' – with some expression of cause – 'because'.

A compound sentence links two or more clauses. The link may be a comma, separating each clause:

> *And the cat with no name <u>sees</u> a flash of cruel teeth,* hears *the angry loud bark of the monster dog, <u>smells</u> the blood and the hunger and the danger.*

It is more usual to link the clauses with a conjunction:

> *David's having a party <u>but</u> it's going to be really bad.*
> *He's only going for 10 days <u>and</u> we're going for two weeks.*

Transposition test

There are only four conjunctions used to form compound sentences:

and, but, so, or.

Pupils could learn these as a list, but it is better to understand their role in structure. The term **co-ordinating conjunction** refers to their function: they operate as simple links, so their position is always *between* two clauses. The test of transposition can demonstrate this and therefore explain the different role of subordinating conjunctions, such as 'because'.

 Go to www.routledge.com/cw/ross for Activity 10.3, Using the transposition test to show the ways that different types of conjunction operate. **Y10+**

Deletion test

The deletion test can be used to demonstrate the different roles of main and subordinate clauses. A **main clause** is one that can stand alone, making complete grammatical sense. This awareness is crucial, if pupils are to punctuate with full stops correctly.

 Go to www.routledge.com/cw/ross for Activity 10.4, Using the deletion test to identify main and subordinate clauses. **Y7+**

Application to punctuation

The role of punctuation marks is to make the sentence structure clear for a reader. The accepted rule was that a comma is required before the conjunctions 'but', 'so' and 'or', but not needed before 'and'. These conventions are changing in contemporary language use. Some writers choose to use commas before 'and'; others no longer use commas before 'but', 'so' and 'or'.

There is some controversy about the use of co-ordinating conjunctions at the beginning of sentences. The familiar rule is:

You should not begin a sentence with <u>and</u> or <u>but</u>.

Pupils should be aware that these conjunctions function as linking words between clauses. Their occasional use at the beginning of a sentence should be a deliberate stylistic choice for emphasis. Orwell, for example, uses this device in his account 'Shooting an Elephant'.

You could see the agony of it jolt his whole body and knock the last remnant of strength from his legs. But in falling he seemed for a moment to rise, for as his hind legs collapsed beneath him he seemed to tower upwards like a huge rock toppling, his trunk reaching skywards like a tree. He trumpeted, for the first and only time. And then down he came, his belly towards me, with a crash that seemed to shake the ground even where I lay.

(Orwell, 'Shooting an Elephant', 1936)

Application to style

Perhaps because the most simple way of linking sentences by 'and' is learnt at an early stage by children, the repeated use of such compound sentences has become a marker of unsophisticated, or childlike expression. The connective 'then' is often used for a similar function. This style may be used deliberately to create an appropriate voice for a narrator, or character, in novels.

 Go to www.routledge.com/cw/ross for Activity 10.5, Identifying the use and effect of compound sentences in fiction. **Y10+**

Complex sentences

It is important for pupils to display competence in handling a variety of complex sentence structures. This section demonstrates the stylistic effects of complex sentences. It shows how pupils can identify subordinate clauses and use two ways of combining these with a main clause. It shows how the position of subordinate clauses can be varied for emphasis.

Glossary

complex sentence   **subordinate clause**   **subordinating conjunction**
non-finite verb   **relative clause**   **embedded clause**   **fronted clause**

Do you like a long sentence that meanders towards the far-off full stop, travelling along the way through subordinate clauses that proliferate, then build up into lists, tropes, asides, tossed-off apercus, always thickening the texture of the paragraph, which it inhabits entirely, and somehow re-enacting the complexity, the density of the experience?

Or do you like a short one?

The areas I have worked in – stand-up comedy, drama and journalism – do not encourage the lengthy, ornate thought. And the world we inhabit accelerates everything, so that every scene is shorter, every image quickly replaced by the next.

(Arthur Smith, The Guardian, 2002)

As Arthur Smith comments in his article, 'ornate' sentence structures are used so rarely nowadays that the modern reader struggles to cope. The first sentence above is extremely complex, combining five, or more, clauses. In language use today, complex sentences are generally restricted to two or three clauses. This still allows the writer to express more complex relationships between the ideas in each clause.

A **complex sentence** combines a main clause with at least one subordinate clause. These subordinate clauses can be connected to the main clause in two ways:

- subordinating conjunctions   'since', 'while', 'that', 'whose', etc.
- non-finite verb forms   'travelling', 'thickening', 'reading', etc.

Transposition test

There are many **subordinating conjunctions**, such as:

> *because, since, although, when, if,*

Although these conjunctions can be learnt as a list, pupils can learn to recognise them by understanding their role in the structure.

The previous section showed how co-ordinating conjunctions – 'and', 'but', 'so', 'or' – function as simple *links*, always operating between two clauses. In contrast, the role of subordinating conjunctions is to *bind* a clause within the overall structure.

Go to www.routledge.com/cw/ross for Activity 10.6, Using the transposition to demonstrate the way that subordinating conjunctions operate. **Y12+**

Deletion test

Subordinate clauses, unlike main clauses, cannot stand alone. The test of deletion can be used to identify subordinate clauses. For example:

> *[Because it is a sunny day], everyone is in the park.*

Go to www.routledge.com/cw/ross for Activity 10.7, Showing a reliable way to identify subordinate clauses. **Y7+**

Relative clauses

The subordinating conjunctions – 'who', 'whom', 'which', 'that' – are grouped together as they introduce a **relative clause**, giving more information about somebody or something. These clauses are often used within the structure of a noun phrase, rather than as a separate clause in the structure of the sentence. The term **embedded clause** refers to the complexity of this structure.

> *He, [<u>whose</u> design includes whatever language can express,] must often speak of what he does not understand.*

> *Do you like a long sentence [<u>that</u> meanders towards the far-off full stop] . . . ?*

Application to punctuation

The use of commas is often explained by reference to pauses or breathing, whereas it would be clearer to consider its role in the structure of a sentence.

Commas are often used to make the boundary between clauses clear to a reader.

> *The world we inhabit accelerates everything, <u>so that</u> every scene is shorter.*

When a conjunction is used *between* clauses, it can be argued that it is a clear structural signpost in itself and needs no further punctuation. Many contemporary writers omit commas in such cases. Orwell, for example, is not consistent, using a comma before 'but' in one sentence, and omitting it in another sentence in the same text.

> *It was obvious that the elephant would never rise again, <u>but</u> he was not dead.*
>
> *At the second shot he did not collapse <u>but</u> climbed with desperate slowness to his feet and stood weakly upright.*

For some reason, it is the accepted convention that no comma is needed before the conjunction 'that', but required before the alternative choice of conjunction 'which'.

> *I realised <u>that</u> it was quite a while since I had read a novel <u>that</u> is largely made up of massive, page-turning sentences.*
>
> *I had read a novel, <u>which</u> is largely made up of massive, page-turning sentences.*

However, a comma is a useful marker, always used when the subordinate clause comes at the beginning of the sentence:

> *<u>When</u> the mind is unchained from necessity, it will range after convenience.*

Non-finite verbs as connectives

Clauses in a complex sentence can also be connected by non-finite verbs. A **non-finite verb** takes two forms:

TABLE 10.2 Non-finite verbs

verb + 'ing'	<u>Rushing</u> out of the house, I forgot to bring my library book.
verb + 'ed'	<u>Bored</u> by the assembly talk, most people stopped listening.
irregular past participle	<u>Driven</u> by ambition, she rose to the top of her profession.

These verb forms are called non-finite as they are 'unfinished', in the sense that they do not make complete grammatical sense. This can be shown by a deletion test. When you remove the main clause, the remaining structure does not make complete sense.

* Rushing out of the house…

* Bored by the assembly talk…

* Driven by ambition…

Like subordinating conjunctions, these connectives remain bound to the clause they introduce. The subordinate clause can be moved to other positions in the sentence structure:

Most people stopped listening, <u>bored</u> by the assembly talk.

She rose to the top of her profession, <u>driven</u> by ambition.

This type of complex sentence structure suggests that the two clauses, or events, are closely related in time. As pupils acquire this structure, they tend to over-use it.

 Go to www.routledge.com/cw/ross for Activity 10.8, Analysing the use and effect of subordinate clauses in 'pulp' fiction. **Y12+**

Applications to style

Although the ability to use complex sentence structures is probably acquired gradually through reading a rich variety of texts, some explicit practice in combining sentences may be useful. Pupils can be asked to revise examples from their own writing. Activity 10.9 provides one example, showing how a sequence of simple sentences may be combined into longer sentence structures. This allows the writer to emphasise particular clauses, by placing them at the beginning of the sentence. The term **fronted clause** is used for this stylistic device.

 Go to www.routledge.com/cw/ross for Activity 10.9, Combining simple sentences into complex sentences. **Y7+**

Adverbial clauses

Subordinate clauses are often referred to as **adverbial clauses**. This is because they function like adverbs or adverbial phrases in significant ways.

- Their role is to add information to the main clause, such as how, when, where or why it happened.
- Like adverbs, these clauses can be deleted or transposed to another position in the structure.

For example, the following clauses express why and when I called out. The brackets indicate that they can be deleted, leaving a complete grammatical structure:

[Unnerved by the strange quiet] [as I walked into the house,] I called out, [fearing that no-one was at home.]

The substitution test shows that subordinate clauses can often be replaced by an adverbial phrase.

 Go to www.routledge.com/cw/ross for Activity 10.10, Showing how subordinate clauses function in the same way as adverbials. **Y12+**

Application to language change

The use of long, complex sentence structures is a common feature of texts from earlier historical periods. Because of this complexity, a variety of punctuation marks are needed as markers between the clauses.

 Go to www.routledge.com/cw/ross for Activity 10.11, Analysing complex sentences. **Y12+**

Application to style

In some genres of writing, it may be appropriate for pupils to use compound sentence structures. A diary entry, for example, is a form of personal writing, where the writer may wish to convey a spontaneous, quasi-spoken voice. The dilemma for teachers, and pupils, is that such writing is still assessed for competence in handling a variety of sentence structures.

 Go to www.routledge.com/cw/ross for Activity 10.12, Analysing the use and effect of different sentence structures in a diary entry (written by a Year 7 pupil). **Y7+**

Application to reading

Awareness of sentence structures can also be applied to reading skills. Pupils should become aware of the ways that a writer's use of varied sentence structure contributes to effects created by vocabulary choice and sound effects.

The final activity uses an extract from a novel. It shows how pupils can use their grammatical knowledge to comment on stylistic effects. Sentence structure works together with vocabulary – the meanings and sound effects of words.

 Go to www.routledge.com/cw/ross for Activity 10.13, Analysing the use and effect of different sentence structures in fiction. **Y10+**

(See Chapter 11 on phonology for further analysis of sound effects in language use).

(See Chapter 12 on semantics for the effects of figurative and emotive vocabulary).

Summary sentence types

Sentences can be classified by their form and function:

- *declarative:*   *subject before verb*   *to make a statement*
- *interrogative:*   *verb before subject*   *to ask a question*
- *imperative:*   *base form of verb*   *to express a command*
- *exclamatory:*   *begins with 'what' or 'how'*   *to express an exclamation*

Sentences can also be classified by their structure:

- *simple:*   *a single main clause*
- *compound:*   *two, or more, main clauses linked*
- *complex:*   *a main clause, combined with two, or more, subordinate clauses*

Clauses are classified into:

- *main:*   *can stand alone; uses a finite verb form*
- *subordinate:*   *cannot stand alone; introduced by: subordinating conjunction, or non-finite verb form (ending in –ing or –ed)*

Subordinate clauses can be identified by the familiar tests:

TABLE 10.3 Tests for subordinate clauses

Deletion	They can be deleted, leaving a complete grammatical structure.
Transposition	Adverbial clauses can be moved to various positions in the structure.
Substitution	Adverbial clauses can be replaced by adverbs or adverbial phrases.

Beyond Grammar

Phonology

This chapter looks at the sounds used to form words in English. Although individual sounds do not have a meaning, there is clearly a shared emotional response to the effects of sounds. Pupils at Key Stage 3 and 4 should be aware of sounds and their effects; for example: vowel, consonant, alliteration, assonance, onomatopoeia.

Pupils grasp these terms quickly and apply them to texts, but often make oversimple observations, such as:

There is alliteration that makes the line flow.

This type of comment suggests that the repetition of any sound conveys the same, rather vague, effect.

This chapter explores intuitive responses: some sounds are perceived as harder or more forceful; others seem softer or more attractive. An understanding of some key terms and concepts from phonology can help pupils comment more precisely on the effects of sounds in poetry and persuasive texts. Awareness of the ways that the sounds of language are produced in the mouth and throat makes the qualities of different types of sounds explicit. However, this explicit knowledge is not required until the study of A-level language.

Further concepts from phonology are introduced for teachers wishing to develop their own understanding. The term 'phoneme' is explained in a brief introductory section. The technical symbols from the International Phonetic Alphabet (IPA) will not be used. Instead, sounds will be represented informally by conventional spelling.

The chapter moves from the study of individual sounds to other features of spoken language: stress, rhythm and intonation. The study of metre in poetry has been covered in many other texts, so is only mentioned in passing. Some examples from the study of rhetoric are included to show the connection between grammatical structure and sound effects.

Sounds and letters

Glossary
sounds   phonemes   vowels   consonants

A moth is not a moth in mother,

Nor both in bother, broth, or brother,

And here is not a match for there,

Nor dear and fear for bear and pear,

And then there's doze and rose and lose –

Just look them up – and goose and choose,

And cork and work and card and ward

And font and front and word and sword,

And do and go and thwart and cart –

Come, I've hardly made a start!

A dreadful language? Man alive!

(author unknown)

This poem makes the important point about the English language that 'sounds and letters don't agree'. One important distinction is between consonants and vowels. Pupils will be familiar with these terms applied to the letters used in writing. However, it is important to be aware that the English alphabet does not correspond exactly to the number of **sounds** used in the language.

The 26 letters of the alphabet suggest that English uses five vowels and 21 consonants. There are, in fact, 44 significant sounds – or **phonemes** – used in spoken English. There are 24 **consonant** phonemes, many of which correspond to a letter of the alphabet:

p, b, t, d, k, g, f, v, s, z, m, n, h, l, r, w

N.B. The phoneme can be represented by the letter 'k' or 'c' or 'ch'.

There are phonemic symbols to represent the remaining consonant sounds, but these can be illustrated using conventional spelling.

ch	*as in*	*church*
dge		*judge*
sh		*sheep*
je		*leisure (this phoneme only occurs in the middle of English words)*
y		*yacht*
ng		*singing (this phoneme only occurs in the middle or end of English words)*
th		*thy*
thigh		*(two phonemes are represented by the letters 'th')*

There are 20 **vowel** phonemes used in the English language, but only five letters in the alphabet. This means that there are many unfamiliar symbols. This technical knowledge is not needed before A-level or degree study. It is sufficient for pupils to be aware that there are more than 5 vowel sounds in English. The section on vowels uses conventional spellings to illustrate the qualities of vowel sounds and their effects.

Consonants

This section explores the emotional effects that certain consonant sounds convey and introduces some terms from phonology to explain the physical basis for these effects.

Glossary
onomatopoeia   consonant   plosive   fricative   nasal   voiced   unvoiced

Sounds U Like

In 1980, the Sunday Times *ran a poll to find out the ten most popular words. They were:*

1. gossamer	*2. crystal*	*3. autumn*	*4. peace*	*5. tranquil*
6. twilight	*7. murmur*	*8. caress*	*9. mellifluous*	*10. whisper*

(www.thetimesonline.co.uk)

Why do people respond favourably to these words? Is it simply the meaning – many refer to delicate properties – or are we influenced by the sound effects as well?

 Go to www.routledge.com/cw/ross for Activity 11.1, Commenting on the sound qualities of the ten most popular words. **Y7+**

Sound effects

The previous activity relied on an impressionistic response to **consonant** sounds – some are perceived as softer, or harder. These effects are used not only in poetry but also in advertising. The sounds used to form words are arbitrary in many ways. Although there are a few examples of **onomatopoeia** in any language – 'clash', 'murmur', 'meow' – the relationship between sound and meaning is usually arbitrary – the sounds *c + a + t* do not represent the type of animal named.

Despite this, there is a sense in which 'sounds have meaning'. In the article in Activity 11.2, the choice of a brand name is influenced by the belief that 'most phonemes have a distinct emotional character'.

Go to www.routledge.com/cw/ross for Activity 11.2, Exploring claims about the effects of certain sounds. **Y9+**

Sound symbolism

As well as the emotional effects mentioned above, there seems to be a relationship between sounds and physical properties.

 Go to www.routledge.com/cw/ross for Activity 11.3, Based on an experiment devised by Kohler (1929). **Y7+**

Application to vocabulary

Although the sound patterns of most words are not related to meaning, certain combinations of sounds occur in groups of words that seem related. For example, the following words all begin with the consonants 'sl':

slack, slouch, sludge, slime, slosh, slash, sloppy, slug, sluggard, slattern, slut, slang, sly, slither, slow, sloth, sleepy, sleet, slip, slipshod, slope, slit, slay, sleek, slant, slovenly, slab, slap, slough, slum, slump, slobber, slaver, slur, slog, slate

According to the linguist Firth (1964), 'A group of words such as the above has a cumulative suggestive value that cannot be overlooked in any consideration of our habits of speech. All the above words are in varying degrees pejorative.'

 Go to www.routledge.com/cw/ross for Activity 11.4, Exploring groups of words with common meanings. **Y7+**

Place and manner of articulation

Why do certain consonant sounds have emotional effects? All consonant sounds are produced by blocking, then releasing, the airflow from the mouth or nose, but there is variation in the way the sounds are produced. Some technical terms from phonology will be introduced to clarify these differences in sound quality. Some details may help pupils explain the effects created by sound in poetry or persuasive writing. Further technical aspects are included for teachers wishing to extend their own understanding.

Plosive sounds

The term **plosive** is used to refer to consonants that are made with 'an explosion of air'. If you say the following sounds, you will notice that they are made by releasing air abruptly from the mouth.

p, b   *t, d*   *k, g*

These consonants have been grouped in pairs to indicate the place of articulation – the position in the mouth.

p,b	*made by closing off the air supply at the lips*
t,d	*made by placing the tongue behind the teeth*
k,g	*made at the back of the mouth*

Pupils should move beyond observing alliteration – the repetition of consonant sounds – to noticing which sounds are repeated and commenting on the emotional effects. Because these plosive sounds come to a stop, they are often associated with emotions such as firmness or determination.

> *Tackling drugs to build a better Britain.*

Perhaps more significant for the effect of these sounds is the aspect of 'voice'. The two sounds in each pair are distinguished by the amount of 'voicing'. If you place your hand over your throat as you say each one, you should notice that the vocal chords vibrate for the **voiced** sounds: *b, d, g*. In advertising, it is suggested that the effect of voiced consonants is more 'luxurious' (Lexicon research group). However, there were few voiced plosive sounds in Activity 11.1.

In contrast, the sounds *p, t, k* are silent, or **unvoiced**. Activity 3 showed that the unvoiced sounds *t* and *k* are associated with an angular shape. An interesting correspondence between sound and meaning is shown in the group of words derived from the root *peuk* (prick):

> *impugn, expunge, pugilist, pugilistic, pygmy, pungent, pounce, poignant, point, puncture, punctuate*

The unvoiced plosive sound *p* is made by the lips and suggests an energetic movement.

Fricative sounds

The term **fricative** refers to the different way other consonants are produced. If you say the following sounds, you will notice that they are made by releasing the air in a 'trickle' from the mouth:

> *th, sh, s, z, f, v*

These sounds can also be grouped in pairs: produced in the same place in the mouth, but with one sound voiced and the other unvoiced. For example, note the difference between the sound in the following pairs of words:

unvoiced	*voiced*	
thigh	*thy*	*(two phonemes represented by the letters 'th')*
fear	*veer*	
Sue	*zoo*	
shack	*Jacques, or the middle sound in 'leisure'*	

Repetition of the *s* or *z* sound, in particular, is often described as 'sibilance'.

> *'There be moe wasps that buzz about his nose.'* (Henry VIII, *Act 3, Scene 2*)

The emotional effect of the unvoiced sounds may be 'softer', with the voiced sounds more 'zippy'. This, perhaps, influenced the choice of brand names with a 'z' sound:

> *Prozac*
>
> *Amazon*

Of course, the associated meanings of other words with the same sound contributes to the appeal. For example, the use of the voiced fricative in the brand name Viagra:

> *Viagra – vitality, vigorous, vital*

Nasal sounds

The term **nasal** refers to consonants produced by releasing air through the nose, rather than the mouth. There are three nasal consonant sounds. One sound only occurs at the end of syllables in English, and is represented by the combination *ng* as in 'singing'.

> *m, n, ng*

If you say these sounds, you will notice that they are voiced. This, and the nasal quality, produces a sonorous effect if a number are used in a text. For example, in these lines from a poem by Tennyson:

> *The moan of doves in immemorial elms, and murmuring of innumerable bees*
>
> (Tennyson, 'The Princess: Come Down, O Maid')

The remaining consonant sounds are made in various ways. They are often perceived as soft, or attractive, sounds. Many occurred in the favourite words in Activity 11.1:

> *l, r, w, y*

Activity 11.3 showed that the sounds *m* and *l* in the word 'maluma' are associated with a rounded shape. Activity 11.5 shows the way these consonant sounds are used for effect in poetry.

Application to poetry

Pupils should be aware of alliteration – the marked repetition of sounds – and begin to make more precise comments about the effects of the *type* of sound used.

 Go to www.routledge.com/cw/ross for Activity 11.5, Analysing the sound effects in poems by Wilfred Owen. **Y10+**

Vowels

There are 20 vowel sounds in English. Whereas consonant sounds are made by blocking the flow of air, vowels are released from an open mouth. Some vowel sounds are short, while others are held for a longer time. The shape of the lips and position of the tongue also changes the sounds made. Although vowel sounds do not *mean* anything in isolation, they appear to convey certain qualities.

 Go to www.routledge.com/cw/ross for Activity 11.6, Based on an experiment devised by the linguist Sapir (1970 [1929]). **Y7+**

Sound symbolism

The previous activity showed that some vowel sounds are associated with physical qualities. Is it convincing to claim that vowel sounds have meaning, in the sense of emotional effects? The following article refers to research into the relative attractiveness of names. Pupils may like to apply these ideas to their own names.

> There is such a thing as a pretty name, some scientists believe, meaning it is good news if you are a Laura or Matt but not so great if you are called Paul or Anne.
>
> Amy Perfors, at Massachussetts Institute of Technology, posted 24 pictures of men and women on a website called Hot or Not. People visiting the site were asked to vote on the attractiveness of the photographs. Every so often she changed the names beneath the pictures to see if it would affect how the votes fell.
>
> She found that the men, when allotted first names such as Nick and Matt, where the stressed vowel is made at the front of the mouth, were voted more attractive than when they were given the name Paul or Charles – where the dominant vowel is made at the back of the throat.
>
> She found it was the reverse for women. Those with names such as Jess and Anne were marked as less attractive than a Julie and Susan.
>
> *(Perfors, 2004)*

This research suggests that certain vowel sounds have a more favourable effect than others, depending on whether the vowel sound is made at the front or back of the mouth. But, for some reason, the response differs according to gender. Perfors sums up her conclusions as follows:

Males, whose names have a vowel sound made at the front of the mouth, are statistically more attractive.

Dave, Craig, Ben, Jake, Rick, Steve, Matt

Those, whose name has a vowel sound made at the back of the mouth, proved less attractive.

Lou, Paul, Luke, Tom, Charles, George, John

The opposite is true for females. Names with a back vowel proved more attractive.

Laura, Julie, Robin, Susan, Holly, Carmen

Female names with a front vowel had a less favourable response.

Melanie, Jamie, Jess, Jill, Amy, Tracy, Ann, Liz

Short v. long vowel sounds

The 20 vowel sounds of English can be grouped in various ways. The example above concentrated on the place of articulation – whether at the front, or back, of the mouth. This aspect, however, is not as obvious as the length of the sound. Vowels can be classified according to whether the sound is short or held for a longer time.

short	long
pit	*peat*
pat	*part*
pot	*port*
pet	*pert*
putt	*poot*
put	

Activity 11.3 showed that the longer vowel sounds in the word 'maluma' are associated with a rounded shape, whereas the shorter sounds in 'takete' suggest an angular shape. Pupils could look again at the vowel sounds repeated in the poems by Wilfred Owen. There are many short vowel sounds in 'Dulce et Decorum Est'; more long vowels are used in 'Exposure'.

The vowels above are all monothongs – single sounds. Some vowel phonemes are dipthongs – slipping from one sound to another. Dipthongs may also convey a richer, rounded effect:

e + I	*as in*	*bay*	
o + I		*boy*	
a + I		*buy*	
a + u		*bough*	
er + u		*bow*	*(ribbon in hair)*
I + er		*beer*	
u + er		*sewer*	
e + er		*hair*	

Attitudes to regional accents

In Received Pronunciation (RP) – the standard – the two words 'put' and 'putt' have a different pronunciation. One feature of Northern regional accents is the use of the same sound for both words. Attitudes to regional accents are often negative, leading some people to take elocution lessons to remove the traces of their accent. These attitudes are softening as regional accents are given prominence in the media. But some stigma is still apparent: RP is used for national news reports, whereas northern accents are used to promote 'homely' products, such as bread, tea and beer.

Rhythm

So far, we have looked at individual sounds and their effects. There are other aspects of spoken language that have an impact on meaning: volume, pitch, stress and intonation. These features are heard in the speaking voice and can be conveyed in writing by visual signs. Punctuation marks, such as commas, full stops and semi-colons, suggest pauses, whereas question and exclamation marks suggest a rising intonation. The use of different fonts and sizes of print can be used for emphasis, often suggesting the intonation of a speaking voice.

Line endings in poetry emphasise rhythmical breaks, sometimes in opposition to the sentence structure of prose. Poetry often uses a regular pattern of stresses – or metre. There are many books that deal with this feature of poetry, so it will not be included here. Instead, some examples are provided to show the rhythmical effects of certain grammatical structures.

Glossary

repetition   parallelism   antithesis

My name is Hinmatuheylocket. I have been asked to show you my heart. I am glad to have a chance to do so now. I want the white man to understand my people. He has many words to tell how my people look to him, but it does not require many words to speak the truth. What I have to say will come from my heart and I will speak it with a straight tongue. The Great Spirit is looking at me and will hear me. I have heard talk and talk, but nothing is done. Good words do not last long until they amount to something. Words do not pay for dead people. They do not pay for my country now overrun with white men. They do not protect my father's grave. They do not pay for my horses and cattle. Good words will not give me back my children. Good words will not give my people good health and stop them from dying. Good words will not get my people a home where they can live in peace and take care of themselves. I am tired of talk that comes to nothing. It makes my heart sick when I remember all the good words and all the broken promises.

(Chief Joseph, 1840–1904)

Repetition

Repetition – whether of individual words or structures – is always marked, in the sense that it is unusual. It is often a deliberate stylistic device for a particular effect. The example above is taken from an old recording of a native American's speech to the US government. Even on the page, the rhythmical effects are moving.

Relatively simple sentence structures and vocabulary combine in a powerful expression of ideals and contradictions. There is marked repetition of 'words' and the related vocabulary, 'speak', 'hear', 'understand'. He contrasts the way words can be used: 'the truth', 'straight tongue', 'from the heart', as opposed to 'broken promises'. Ironically the phrase 'good words' is linked with the 'broken promises'. This is emphasised by the repetition of similar sentence structures, beginning with 'They do not...' Words are contrasted with actions, by the juxtaposition 'I have heard talk and talk, but nothing is done'.

The study of rhetoric provides technical terms for different types of repetition, but few of these terms are in common use today. The following examples from a website on rhetoric illustrate various types of repetition used by Shakespeare.

Parallelism: Similarity of structure in a pair or series of related words, phrases, or clauses:

> *And therefore, since I cannot prove a lover*
>
> *To entertain these fair well-spoken days,*
>
> *I am determinèd to prove a villain*
>
> *And hate the idle pleasures of these days.*

> *(Richard III, Act 1, Scene 1)*

antithesis: Juxtaposition, or contrast of ideas or words in a balanced or parallel construction

> *Not that I loved Caesar less, but that I loved Rome more.*

> *(Julius Caesar, Act 3, Scene 2)*

The repetition of a word that ends one clause at the beginning of the next:

> *My conscience hath a thousand several tongues,*
>
> *And every tongue brings in a several tale,*
>
> *And every tale condemns me for a villain.*

> *(Richard III, Act 5, Scene 2)*

Repetition of a word or phrase as the beginning of successive clauses:

> *Mad world! Mad kings! Mad composition!*

> *(King John, Act 2, Scene 1)*

Two corresponding pairs arranged in a parallel inverse order:

Fair is foul, and foul is fair

(*Macbeth*, Act 1, Scene 1)

Repetition broken up by one or more intervening words:

Put out the light, and then put out the light.

(*Othello*, Act 5, Scene 2)

Repetition at the end of a clause of the word that occurred at the beginning of the clause:

Blood hath bought blood, and blows have answer'd blows.

(*King John*, Act 2, Scene 1)

Frequent repetition of a phrase or question, dwelling on a point:

Who is here so base that would be a bondman? If any, speak; for him I have offended. Who is here so rude that would not be a Roman? If any speak; for him have I offended.

(*Julius Caesar*, Act 3, Scene 2)

Repetition of a word or phrase at the end of successive clauses:

I'll have my bond!

Speak not against my bond!

I have sworn an oath that I will have my bond.

(*Merchant of Venice*, Act 3, Scene 3)

Altering word order, or separation of words that belong together, for emphasis:

Some rise by sin, and some by virtue fall.

(*Measure for Measure*, Act 2, Scene 1)

The repetition of conjunctions in a series of co-ordinate words, phrases, or clauses:

If there be cords, or knives,

Poison, or fire, or suffocating streams,

I'll not endure it.

(*Othello*, Act 3, Scene 3)

 Go to www.routledge.com/cw/ross for Activity 11.7, Analysing the rhetorical features in a speech. **Y10+**

Balanced structures

The use of balanced structures is a feature of memorable sayings. Perhaps this type of structure suggests that the ideas are related, as strongly as a mathematical formula.

> *The eyes of others are our prisons; their thoughts our cages.*
>
>

(Virginia Woolf)

eyes	=	*prisons*
thoughts	=	*cages*

> *Every society honours its live conformists and its dead troublemakers.*
>
>

(Mignon McLaughlin)

live	*v.*	*dead*
conformists	*v.*	*troublemakers*
yet:		
dead troublemaker	=	*live conformist (both honoured by society)*

The use of a triple structure has always proved effective, its rhythm suggesting a build-up to a climax:

> *Men in great place are thrice servants: servants of the sovereign or state; servants of fame; and servants of business.*
>
>

(Francis Bacon)

Often, this device is extended to a list of three, or four items.

> *One equal temper of heroic hearts,*
>
> *Made weak by time and fate, but strong in will*
>
> *To strive, to seek, to find, and not to yield.*
>
>

(Tennyson, 'Ulysses')

This chapter concludes with an activity that asks pupils to notice the combination of individual sounds with rhythmical grammatical structures.

 Go to www.routledge.com/cw/ross for Activity 11.8, Analysing the use and effect of rhetorical features in political speeches.

The next chapter moves onto the questions of meaning. It introduces some useful concepts from the study of semantics into the relationship between words and meanings.

Semantics

This chapter moves away from the structural features of language to explore the ways that words convey meanings. This area will be familiar to readers with a background in literature study. The key concept is 'figurative' language. Pupils quickly learn to use the terms – metaphor, simile, connotation – to *describe* features of texts, but need to show a subtle understanding of the effects.

The study of semantics is an area where the disciplines of linguistics, literature, communication and cultural studies come together. It offers some useful concepts to develop pupils' awareness of the effects of vocabulary choice. The chapter begins with the most straightforward understanding of vocabulary – its 'literal' meaning. But a living language is rarely so straightforward.

From a large vocabulary store, words can be chosen, not simply to communicate facts, but also to convey subtle shades of meaning, with underlying emotional effects or attitudes. The concept of emotive vocabulary is explored, introducing the terms 'collocation' and 'juxtaposition'. The ways that words occur in combination has an effect on their associated meanings.

Activities encourage pupils to use dictionaries to explore the etymology of words to see how meanings may change over time. It is important for pupils to notice shifts in meaning from the literal to the 'metaphorical'.

Poetry is often difficult – and rewarding – because of its use of fresh combinations of words, images and ideas. Examples of non-literary texts encourage pupils to become aware that metaphors are common – and significant – in everyday language.

The relationship between words and meaning

This opening section explores some ideas about the way words express meanings. On the one hand, there is the attitude that words are harmless: 'Sticks and stones may break my bones, but words can never harm me.' And yet, many people feel that it really does make a difference what words are used, that groups of people can be harmed by the words used to refer to them.

Glossary
literal   denotation   synonym v. antonym

> *I pray thee, understand a plain man in his plain meaning*
>
> (*Shakespeare*, Merchant of Venice)
>
> *When I use a word… it means just what I choose it to mean – neither more nor less.*
>
> (*Carroll*, Through the Looking Glass)
>
> *The purpose of Newspeak was not only to provide a medium of expression for the world-view and mental habits proper to the devotees of IngSoc, but to make all other modes of thought impossible.*
>
> (*Orwell*, Nineteen Eighty-four)
>
> *That which we call a rose by any other name would smell as sweet.*
>
> (*Shakespeare*, Romeo and Juliet)

Does it matter what word we choose?

The quotations above introduce the discussion of words and meanings. The first suggests the 'common-sense' view that a word stands for something in the outside world. If this is the case, words can be used to express a 'plain' meaning, with no ambiguity or extra dimensions. But Lewis Carroll's character Humpty Dumpty makes a claim that seems absurd – surely all language users must use words to mean the same thing in order to communicate?

Can words *control* thought, so that it is impossible to have an idea for which no word exists? This is what Orwell's fictional language of Newspeak attempted to achieve – by ridding the language of words for undesirable concepts, the rulers hoped to eradicate such thoughts. The Sapir-Whorff hypothesis seems to support this view of words and meanings, suggesting that our perception of the world is affected – or even controlled – by the words we have to describe it. The example, often quoted but now considered misleading, is of the many words for 'snow' in the language of Eskimos. According to this argument, English language users cannot perceive subtly different types of snow because we do not have the words in our vocabulary.

Does it make any difference what name is given to something? Would a rose 'smell as sweet' even if it was called a 'spludge' or 'wonkle'? As the previous chapter on Phonology showed, naming can be significant. My alternative words certainly lack the pleasant sounds in the word 'rose', but perhaps other words would serve as well to name this flower. The movement, mocked by its opponents as 'political correctness', pointed out the negative effects of labelling people with disabilities as 'cripples', referring to people of African origin as 'coloured' and calling any females 'girls'.

Pupils should become aware of the power of words to do more than simply represent things in a neutral way. The semantic concepts of denotation, synonym, antonym, connotation and collocation can be used to explore the complex relationships between words and meanings.

Denotation

The starting point in semantics is the concept of **denotation**. This term refers to the most straightforward relationship between a word and its meaning: a word stands for the object in the world that it represents. This relationship could be expressed by an equals sign, so that the word 'chair' = an object with four legs and a back. Dictionary definitions attempt to supply the denotative meanings of words, using **synonyms** or brief explanations:

> *chair, a separate seat for one person, usually having a back and four legs*

This is the **literal** meaning of the word 'chair'. But even this simple word has acquired further meanings: a seat of authority; the person holding that position; to carry a person aloft in triumph. The concept of metaphorical extension of meaning is explored in a later section.

With concrete nouns this relationship – a word denotes a specific aspect of the world – is reasonably convincing. But the meaning of abstract concepts is not so straightforward. Perhaps, like Humpty Dumpty, each person uses abstract words to mean 'just what I choose it to mean'.

 Go to www.routledge.com/cw/ross for Activity 12.1, Exploring the meanings of the word *love*. **Y9+**

The next section looks at ways that words acquire associated meanings.

Emotive language

Glossary
emotive language   connotation   collocation   juxtaposition   etymology

---

I am firm, you are stubborn, and he is pig-headed.

(George Bernard Shaw)

| *pro-choice* | *or* | *baby killers* |
| *collateral damage* | *or* | *civilian casualties* |

The vocabulary of the English language has hundreds of thousands of words. As the examples above show, there are often various choices of words for a single concept. The first list of three could be extended further:

> *unyielding, determined, resolute, dogged, tenacious, obdurate, uncompromising, intransigent, mulish*

A thesaurus is a useful reference source for words related in meaning. The ability to vary the choice of vocabulary is an important skill, but pupils should be aware that these apparent synonyms do not simply convey a denotative meaning; words also acquire **emotive** meanings.

When talking about abortion, for example, the terms 'pro-choice' and 'baby killers' may denote the same thing, but from a very different viewpoint. Our vocabulary provides euphemisms to mask the harsh reality of taboo subjects, such as death, as in the vaguely detached reference to 'collateral damage'. Even the phrase 'civilian casualties' avoids the mention of death or connotations of outrage and blame, as might be found in a more emotive phrasing: 'the murder of innocent women and children'. The concept of connotation is a significant aspect of the meanings of words, particularly when grouping words as synonyms or antonyms.

Connotations

Although such groups of words can be termed synonyms, it is difficult to claim that they have the *same* meaning. As well as the literal, dictionary definition, each word has acquired slightly different associations, or emotive effects. The term **connotation** is used to distinguish the denotation of the word from its emotive meanings. There are many alternative words, for example, to denote mental illness:

> *mad, crazy, insane, deranged,* etc.

Some terms are intended to convey a neutral description; others are derogatory. When the boxer Frank Bruno was admitted to hospital, the early editions of the *Sun* newspaper carried the headline 'Bonkers Bruno'. The public reaction was clearly far more sympathetic, and later editions were quickly changed to 'Sad Bruno in Hospital'.

Etymology – word origins

Pupils should be aware that apparent synonyms carry emotive overtones. Such shades of meaning are acquired in their use over time, but can be explained partly by their **etymology**: their language origin. The main sources of English vocabulary are Anglo-Saxon, Latin and French. The vocabulary of Old English was Anglo-Saxon; the successive influences of Latin and French did not replace the original words, but added alternatives. In contemporary English, there are often at least three choices for a single concept:

Old English	French	Latin
kingly	*royal*	*regal*
killing	*murder*	*homicide*

However, these words are not simply interchangeable. They may simply occur in different contexts. The word 'kingly' is rarely used in modern English, so has an archaic flavour.

Thou who, in all Thy mighty, earthly marchings, ever cullest Thy selectest champions from the kingly commons; bear me out in it, O God!

(*Melville*, Moby-Dick)

The word 'regal' tends to be used in brand names: Regal cinema/hotel, etc., or to describe a haughty manner. The word 'royal' has become the accepted term for describing the position of a monarchy.

The different words to refer to deliberate taking of a person's life are all in use today, but when one is substituted for another, different shades of meaning are conveyed. Ian Brady is described in the media as the 'Moors *murderer*'. He, however, describes his activities as 'periodic *homicide*', choosing a word derived from Latin, with more abstract, legal connotations. The Old English word *'killing'* is perhaps too blunt to be mentioned.

Go to www.routledge.com/cw/ross for Activity 12.2, Exploring the connotations of synonyms. **Y7+**

Collocation

The term **collocation** refers to 'the habitual co-occurrence of words'. In other words, its regular use in certain contexts. The fact that certain words often occur together affects their associated emotive meanings. For example, because the word 'chubby' is often used to describe children, it has more positive overtones of health. The term 'obese' tends to be used in medical contexts, combined with terms such as 'diabetes' or 'heart disease', so has acquired more formal, negative connotations. The choice of one synonym rather than another is therefore not an arbitrary choice. The plain, denotative sense of the word includes various associated meanings, often connected with memories of previous uses, or collocations.

Go to www.routledge.com/cw/ross for Activity 12.3, Exploring the collocations and connotations of the word *swamp*. **Y12+**

Underlying attitudes and values

Pupils should be sensitive to the emotive associations of words. Politicians, for example, are often accused of 'spin'. This image suggests that their choice of words is not a straightforward representation but a way of disguising some underlying attitudes. When the Home Secretary David Blunkett suggested that children of asylum seekers should be provided with separate education to avoid local schools being swamped, critics objected to his juxtaposition of the word 'swamped' with 'asylum-seekers'. His response was that this reaction was 'oversensitive'. Perhaps, like Humpty Dumpty, he used this word to mean no more than a larger number than could be handled; he wanted it to be understood in its 'plain' meaning. But the word 'swamp' has acquired further connotations. It regularly occurs in combination with asylum seekers, notably in hostile contexts. It is used in media headlines:

Influx of asylum-seekers threatening to swamp the UK

The image suggested by 'influx' relates the waters of a swamp to the powerful movement of the sea. This was used in a National Front newsletter (2001), which referred to a 'flood tide of bogus asylum-seekers'. This, in turn, may recall the image of 'rivers of blood' used in a famous speech by Enoch Powell in 1968, when he said:

'like the Roman, I seem to see the River Tiber foaming with much blood'.

It is not only politicians who can imply underlying attitudes by their choice of vocabulary. In a radio programme about transsexuals, one speaker commented that now that the laws have become more liberal, 'more are coming out of the woodwork'. His attitude was not overtly hostile, but his choice of words suggests an underlying fear. Words for pests and insects, such as cockroaches are often found in collocation with the phrase 'out of the woodwork'.

The use of words with negative connotations is often a feature of persuasive language, where the speaker, or writer, wants to convey a feeling of threat. Tony Blair needed to justify his decision to declare war on Iraq, so, in a public speech, he used words such as 'systematically raped, pillaged, and plundered a tiny nation'; 'maimed and murdered, innocent children'. Other texts may present their point of view in more subtle ways.

 Go to www.routledge.com/cw/ross for Activity 12.4, Analysing the use of emotive language in a media article on 'drinking'. **Y10+**

Juxtaposition

The literary term **juxtaposition** is similar to the concept of collocation, but it refers to particular instances of unusual combinations. This creative use of vocabulary is often a feature of poetry. The phrase *a grief ago* (Dylan Thomas) uses the abstract noun *grief* in the usual place of words for time: *minute, year,* etc. The reader must work out a connection, in order to understand this new idea. The juxtaposition emphasises the incalculable length of time that grief lasts.

 Go to www.routledge.com/cw/ross for Activity 12.5, Analysing the effect of juxtaposition in a poem. **Y10+**

Figurative language

figurative language   images   imagery   metaphor   simile   metonym
symbol   personification

> *This article is called 'Tall Stories' because in it I want to look at some of the stories we have in our heads about what talk is like, and ask whether they are true or not. More particularly, I want to question one of the tallest stories we have in our culture about talk – and that is that the everyday variety is a transparent medium, a bit of a metaphor-free zone.*
>
> *In fact, research has been discovering that our everyday discourse is highly metaphorical, and metaphorical in systematic ways that relate to the way we think and behave. In order to show this, I want to look at the nature of the metaphors we use as our common currency, and ask some questions about what our everyday metaphors say about us.*
>
> *(Goddard, Tall Stories: The Metaphorical Nature of Everyday Talk, 1996)*

This article explodes a common myth that figurative language – metaphors in particular – is only used in literary texts. Pupils should be aware of this use of language in all texts.

As Goddard observes, metaphors in everyday language tend to pass unnoticed. Perhaps these metaphors from the extract were 'invisible': 'tall stories'; 'looking at metaphor'; 'talk as a zone'; 'talk as money'; and metaphors as 'people'.

The phrase **figurative language** is the overall term for the extension of meaning from the literal to the metaphorical. This 'umbrella' term includes various devices for conveying non-literal meanings: simile, symbol, metonym, metaphor. The first two are so familiar that a brief comment is provided. Although the term 'metonym' is not explicitly required, an activity demonstrates that pupils are aware of this device for conveying implied meanings. Metaphors are explored in detail later.

The term **simile** is used for explicit comparisons, when the words 'like' or 'as' are used:

> *My love is like a red, red rose. (Burns)*
>
> *I felt as sick as a parrot.*

These are simple to identify, but pupils should notice whether the simile is effective. Some have become clichés; others may be unconvincing or strange.

> *The pleasure hit me like a runaway baboon*
>
> *('Haagen-Dazs ice-cream' advertisement)*
>
> *Eyebrows like caterpillars on the tree of knowledge*   (Saul Bellow)

The term **symbol** is used for a sign that stands for something in a particular social community. Colours, for example, acquire symbolic meanings: black for death, red for danger or passion, white for purity, etc. These symbolic meanings may vary from culture to culture, or over time.

The term **metonym** is used when an attribute is used to represent the whole, as in:

> *The keel (ship) ploughed the waves (sea).*
>
> *The crown (title of king) passed to Prince Harry.*

Pupils should notice the way certain physical aspects are used to represent general characteristics. Such meanings are often specific to a particular social context. In contemporary language, these attributes are used to suggest a particular type of person, or lifestyle:

> *white-van man*
>
> *Essex girls*
>
> *bling*

 Go to www.routledge.com/cw/ross for Activity 12.6, Using creative writing to explore pupils' implicit awareness of metonyms. **Y12+**

Dead metaphors

A **metaphor**, like these other figurative uses of words, suggests a connection, usually between a physical entity and an abstract idea. Unusual metaphors draw attention to themselves, but many have become so familiar, that they may pass unnoticed.

Many common words in the language began as metaphors, but the literal meaning has been forgotten. A person described as 'keen' on sport, or having a 'keen' interest in science, is understood to be enthusiastic; the original meaning of 'sharp', as in 'keen' weapons, is no longer used. The term 'dead metaphor' is used for such examples. Any fairly large (Concise) dictionary provides details of the word's derivation in square brackets at the end. For example, the word 'muscle' derives from the Latin word *musculus* meaning 'mouse'.

 Go to www.routledge.com/cw/ross for Activity 12.7, Using dictionaries to explore examples of the ways that meanings change over time. **Y10+**

Images

The term **imagery** is often used as an alternative for 'figurative language', as abstract ideas are often conveyed by visual **images**. Imagery may also use the other physical senses of hearing, touch, taste and smell.

Go to www.routledge.com/cw/ross for Activity 12.8, Collecting examples of figurative language in common use.

Spatial images

Spatial concepts are often used in figurative senses. We talk of getting ahead or falling behind; feeling high or low; including people or leaving them out. Pupils might collect common expressions connected to these physical positions:

> *up v. down*
>
> *in front v. behind*
>
> *inside v. outside*

Implied attitudes

These spatial metaphors are probably shared by all cultures – it is unlikely that the figurative sense of 'down' or 'outside' could have positive associations. However, some metaphorical uses of language may reflect the attitudes and values of a particular social group. A Saudi Arabian student commented on the strange amount of freedom women were permitted in our culture, saying 'My wife is like gold. I keep her in a box.' This metaphor may seem repressive, but there are related metaphors of possession in contemporary discourse about male/female relationships: 'bonds', 'ties', 'to have and to hold', etc.

Go to www.routledge.com/cw/ross for Activity 12.9, Exploring the figurative language used to convey ideas above love and relationships. **Y10+**

Application to language change

Colloquial expressions about love and relationships may change over time. The image of 'being left on the shelf' seems rather old-fashioned in its negative attitude to a life outside a relationship, but the more modern expression 'dumped' is even more despairing. Problem pages are a source of contemporary figurative language about love and relationships.

Go to www.routledge.com/cw/ross for Activity 12.10, Analysing the use and effect of metaphors about love in problem-page letters. **Y10+**

Application to literary texts

There are so many ready-made phrases to describe emotions that it is hard to find a way to make such clichés 'come to life'. In literary texts, a familiar metaphor is often developed in unusual ways. For example, 'My legs turned to jelly' is made fresh by

D.H. Lawrence (*Monkey Nuts*):

> *Her arm was around his waist, she drew him closely to her with a soft pressure that made his bones rotten*

 Go to www.routledge.com/cw/ross for Activity 12.11, Comparing familiar clichés about love with metaphors used in literary texts. **Y10+**

Integrating grammar and semantics

This area of semantics plays to the strengths of teachers with a literary background. Pupils' understanding of ways meanings are conveyed remains central to language study.

 Go to www.routledge.com/cw/ross for Activity 12.12, Analysing the use and effects of both grammatical structures and use of figurative language in a literary text. **Y12+**

The next chapters look at the area of discourse studies, introducing terms and concepts for the study of whole texts in their social context.

Discourse

The final chapters move on to the study of whole texts. The progression of chapters in the book mirrors the organisation of language study into the three levels of Word, Sentence and Text.

TABLE 13.1 Chapter topics

	Word	Sentence	Text
Chapters 2 and 3	morphology		
Chapters 4–10		syntax	
Chapter 11	phonology		
Chapter 12	semantics		
Chapter 13			discourse
Chapter 14			spoken language
Chapter 15			electronic modes

This chapter introduces some useful, accessible concepts from the study of 'discourse'. This term signals a shift in interest: from words and sentences in isolation to the way language works in its full context. This may come as a relief to those sceptical about the value of a 'microscopic' analysis of language. Many aspects of discourse studies are familiar to teachers with a background in literature study.

genre	*forms*	*text types*
context	*situation*	*circumstances*
register	*formality*	

The first section explores the structure of written texts – the ways links between paragraphs are signposted.

The key concepts of genre, purpose and audience are used to develop pupils' awareness of context.

The concept of register is used to explore the ways that language varies according to the context.

Some activities explore the conventions associated with different genres and the effects of innovation.

Text structure

losing the thread

tying up loose ends

cotton on

spin a yarn

The phrases above show the metaphor of woven cloth recurring as an image for language use. Although individual sentences may be well constructed, they need to be connected to each other in ways that aid comprehension of the overall argument. They need to cohere – or stick together.

In everyday use, the words 'discourse' and 'text' are used to mean, respectively, talking and writing. Yet the two concepts are closely related. The Latin root of the term 'discourse' comes from the word *discursus*, meaning to run; the Latin root of the term 'text' comes from *texere*, meaning to weave. Speakers and writers may 'run on and on', but effective speech and writing requires clear patterning, rather like the construction of material from loose threads.

Cohesion

There are two types of **cohesion**: lexical and grammatical. In the former, the use of related vocabulary items form the threads that weave a text into a coherent whole. In the latter, use of pronouns and connectives indicate the links between sentences.

Lexical cohesion

direct repetition:	e.g. the word *creature*
synonyms:	e.g. *creature / animal / being*
antonyms:	e.g. *animate v. non-animate*
super-ordination:	e.g. *creature – reptile – snake – python*
specific-general reference:	e.g. *snake – poisonous snake, pet snake*

N.B. The technical term 'super-ordination' refers to a hierarchy of terms, so that a general term such as 'food' includes many sub-categories, including 'pasta', which can be further specified into types, such as macaroni. Specific types of macaroni can be named: 'quick cook', 'wholewheat', etc. This relationship is termed 'specific-general reference'.

Grammatical cohesion

pronoun reference:	e.g. *snakes: it, they,*
connectives:	e.g. *for example, on the other hand*
linking phrases:	e.g. *in the desert, in many cases*
reference back:	e.g. *such snakes, these snakes*

Go to www.routledge.com/cw/ross or Activity 13.1, Identifying cohesive devises. **Y10+**

Discourse markers

The single paragraph in Activity 13.1 used various devices to make it cohesive. Pupils also need to recognise and use a range of connectives between paragraphs.

N.B. Such devices are also termed 'discourse markers' or 'transition devices'. There is useful material on transition devices on various websites. (www.sdc.uwo.ca/writing/handouts).

Key connectives (discourse markers) can be grouped by their function. For example:

addition	*also, furthermore, moreover*
opposition	*however, nevertheless, on the other hand*

Activities based on jumbled paragraphs can make pupils aware of the way texts are organised. The individual paragraphs of a text can be cut up and rearranged. If the text is cohesive, it should be possible to work out the original sequence of paragraphs. Pupils may be asked to add connectives to signpost the links between paragraphs.

Written texts can use visual markers, other than paragraph breaks, to signpost their structure. Talks and other spoken presentations need to use aural clues, such as pauses, stress and intonation, to highlight the verbal markers of structure.

Go to www.routledge.com/cw/ross for Activity 13.2, Comparing the use of discourse markers in written and spoken texts. **Y12+**

Register – degrees of formality

Glossary
register   formality   situation/context   setting   audience/participants
purpose   topic   genre

> *No smoking*
>
> *Stub it out!*
>
> *Smoking is not permitted,*
>
> *Please refrain from smoking,*
>
> *Your co-operation in refraining from smoking is appreciated,*
>
> *Patrons are respectfully reminded that smoking is not allowed on these premises.*

The term **register** is borrowed from the field of music and refers to the varying degrees of formality that may be conveyed in language. As the examples above show, the 'no-smoking' message can be expressed in various ways, depending on the situation. Choice of vocabulary and sentence structures affects the degree of **formality** of the message.

 Go to www.routledge.com/cw/ross for Activity 13.3, Analysing the levels of formality in the 'no-smoking' notices above. **Y8+**

Situation of language use

A brief definition of **register** is:

> *The way language varies according to situation*

The alternative term 'formality' is often used, but pupils should be aware that this does not refer to a simple distinction between two styles of language: formal v. informal. The notion of *degrees* of formality is important, so that language use can be seen as a subtle continuum, ranging from the most formal, impersonal style through to the most personal, informal style of communication between close friends. It is obvious that one significant aspect of language use is the people involved and their relationship. This may be the writer and reader, or readers; the speaker and their audience, or the participants in a two-way conversation. But there are other aspects of the situation that influence the register. The following framework (Holmes, 1992) suggests that the **situation** includes these four social factors and dimensions:

Factor	Dimension
participants	*social distance*
	social status
purpose	*function*
topic	
setting	*formality*

This is similar to the concepts used in the classroom, sometimes abbreviated to acronyms such as GAP or SPAG, which refer to the familiar terms:

subject	*(topic)*
purpose	
audience	*(participants)*
genre	

This framework includes the extra factor of the **genre** of language used. The two main divisions between the modes of **spoken** and **written** language use can each be divided into more specific types, or forms, of language use: a spoken conversation or scripted speech; a written letter, notice, leaflet, report, review, narrative, poem, etc. This shorthand version of the context – or situation – is useful as an *aide-memoire* for pupils, but needs to be used with some subtlety. It is not enough to 'pigeonhole' a text with four simple labels.

 Go to www.routledge.com/cw/ross for Activity 13.4, Encouraging a more subtle account of the context and register of texts. **Y12+**

Extending analysis of register

Even this analysis (commentary for Activity 13.4) overlooks the complexity of the register, which actually shifts between informal and more formal, in order to achieve the desired effect.

Pupils should think of the purposes (in the plural) of language use, and develop the concept of audience to include the relationship, or interaction between writer and reader. The following framework of concepts may be useful, each represented as a continuum:

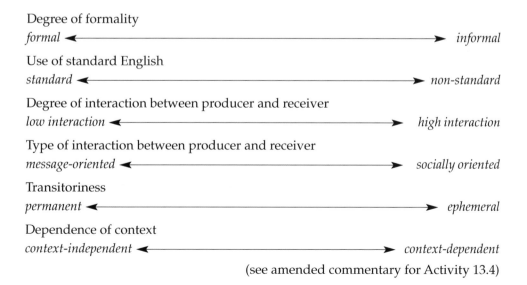

Degree of formality
formal ◄————————————————————————► *informal*

Use of standard English
standard ◄————————————————————————► *non-standard*

Degree of interaction between producer and receiver
low interaction ◄————————————————————————► *high interaction*

Type of interaction between producer and receiver
message-oriented ◄————————————————————————► *socially oriented*

Transitoriness
permanent ◄————————————————————————► *ephemeral*

Dependence of context
context-independent ◄————————————————————————► *context-dependent*

(see amended commentary for Activity 13.4)

Application to writing skills

Pupils can transfer this awareness of the register of texts to their own language use.

 Go to www.routledge.com/cw/ross for Activity 13.5, Creating and evaluating texts for a particular purpose and audience. **Y8+**

Degrees of formality in language

It is helpful to isolate one or two factors of language in use in order to focus on subtle differences. Teachers could collect a group of texts, all of a similar genre, but with significant differences of purpose and audience. If the texts are produced on individual cards, pupils can work in groups, ranking them in a scale of formality and discussing possible alternatives. This intuitive awareness can be developed by explaining the significant factors of each situation. The identification of purpose and audience should be extended, using some of the concepts suggested above. Pupils should then identify some features of language use that convey the appropriate degree of formality. The following language features are often markers of the degree of formality:

Formal	*Informal*
	Word choice
standard English	*non-standard, colloquial, slang, abbreviations*
polysyllabic words	*monosyllabic words*
Latinate vocabulary	*vocabulary of Anglo-Saxon origin*
	Syntax
complex structures	*non-standard and simple structures*
impersonal address	*direct address with first and second person pronouns*
passive voice	*interrogatives and imperative structures*

 Go to www.routledge.com/cw/ross for Activity 13.6, Ranking short texts according to degree of formality. **Y12+**

Implied meanings

An awareness of register can help pupils identify implied meanings in texts. A high degree of formality often conveys a position of authority for the writer and a corresponding lack of status for the audience. An informal style often suggests an equal relationship between writer and audience.

Pupils need to be aware of these implications of the degree of formality they adopt. The flyer addressed to neighbours in Activity 13.6 manages to combine politeness with friendliness. In some situations, the reader may feel patronised if the tone seems inappropriate. The advice leaflet on bullying (Activity 13.3) uses a formal style to address teachers, suggesting a position of authority, although the writer is a pupil.

There is a trend towards increasing informality in many contexts of contemporary language use. Perhaps this reflects more democratic, equal relationships in today's society. People are often addressed by first name – often to the dismay of older people – and the use of colloquial vocabulary, or even slang, is common in broadsheet newspapers, political speeches and academic texts. Pupils should be aware of this, but it is safer to err on the side of caution in public forms of language, where the audience is outside their familiar sphere, or the purpose is serious. It is not appropriate, for example, to refer to authors by their first name alone in essays: it may be 'Jane Austen', or 'Austen', but never 'Jane'.

Purpose and audience

In the secondary-English curriculum, pupils need to practise writing for a range of different purposes and audiences:

- to inform, explain, describe
- to persuade, argue, advise
- to analyse, review, comment
- to imagine, explore, entertain.

This neat outline may suggest that it is straightforward to distinguish the purpose of any piece of writing and the style needed. But writing to entertain takes many forms. By its nature, imaginative writing is innovative, so exposure to a range of literary, non-fiction texts provides pupils with ideas for their own writing.

Some overtly persuasive texts do have the features listed (in the standards.dfes website):

> *emphasises key points and articulates logical links in the argument*

However, many writers convey their point of view with a mixture of information and entertainment.

Perhaps it is easier to identify the main stylistic conventions of informative and instructional texts (*ibid.*):

> **information**, *which maintains the use of the present tense and the third person, organises and links information clearly; incorporates examples*
>
> **instructions**, *which are helpfully sequenced and signposted, deploy imperative verbs and provide clear guidance.*

Examples of texts written for these purposes can be used as models for pupils' own writing. Their understanding of grammatical terms and concepts can be applied in reading the text and then in redrafting their own work.

Go to www.routledge.com/cw/ross for Activity 13.7, Comparing the register of informative texts with different audiences. **Y10+**

Genre

In the study of discourse, **genre** is defined as 'the stylistic characteristics associated with a particular form of language'. Pupils need to become aware of the conventions of a variety of genres outside their immediate social experience, so that they do not use inappropriate forms, often those of informal conversations, emails or text-messaging.

---

1   *Good morning everybody...*
       I want to see how QUIETLY you can all leave.

2   *All rise...*
       The session is now adjourned.

3   *Dear Occupier...*
       Apply now if you wish to claim your place in the prize draw.

4   *It was a dark and stormy night and the brigands were there...*
       The villagers could now live in peace.

The way a text opens and closes often provides a clear indication of its genre. Teachers could provide pupils with the first and last sentence of a variety of texts and ask them to identify the genre. The examples above follow the expected conventions of:

- spoken: a junior school assembly;
- spoken: court proceedings;
- written: junk mail promotion;
- written or spoken: narrative.

Innovation in language use

An awareness of genre is an important part of a reader's competence – any text is interpreted within a framework of our expectations of language use. Of course, the conventions are not absolutely fixed, so pupils should also notice deviations from the expected norm, or cross-over between genres.

Go to www.routledge.com/cw/ross for Activity 13.8, Analysing texts that subvert the usual conventions of the genre. **Y12+**

New genres

The conventions for new genres are emerging through use. In the case of emails, for example, perhaps it is the older generation, that needs to learn the ways these differ from letters.

(See Chapter 15 on Electronic modes).

 Go to www.routledge.com/cw/ross for Activity 13.9, Exploring the variety of conventions used in the genre of emails. **Y12+**

The final two chapters look in more detail at spoken language and electronic modes of language.

Spoken language

Spoken language is now an important part of English language study, with new units introduced at GCSE, as well as the existing A-level Language specifications. Now that it's cheap and simple to record speech – on mobile phones as well as digital recorders – there is much more data to investigate. There are various corpora (collections) of spoken English available on the internet, with several millions of words taken from a variety of sources, formal and informal, different age groups, social and regional backgrounds.

When people relied on their general impression of what spoken language was like, they tended to compare it unfavourably with written language. It seemed less well organised, not as precise. Some familiar grammatical structures of writing were abbreviated or unfinished. Now the focus is on the particular nature of spoken language and its resulting distinctive forms.

The nature of spoken language

Glossary
channel   mode   turn-taking   deixis   interrogative   imperative

Messages can be communicated – in any language – via different **channels**:

- Braille uses touch   with raised dots on a page
- sign language uses sight   with hand gestures
- written language also uses sight   with marks on paper
- spoken language uses hearing   with sounds

This physical aspect of communication obviously has an effect, but other factors are probably more significant. Speech, like sign language, is essentially an interactive **mode** of communication. It usually takes place face-to-face, in real time. Writing and Braille, on the other hand, tend to be created and then read alone, with a distance and a time lag between writer and reader.

This interactive nature of spoken language accounts for two distinctive features: **turn-taking** and **deixis**. Speech usually has the form of a dialogue, weaving together turns from the participants. Speakers address each other directly using more **interrogatives** (questions) and **imperatives** (commands, requests, instructions) than in written language. As the speakers are co-present in a particular situation, it is possible to refer to the context without having to use explicit names. An utterance such as the following would make little sense in writing:

Can you chuck it over there for that lad?

The term 'deixis' comes from the Greek for the index, or pointing finger, as they 'point' the listener to something outside the sentence. Deictic terms are usually grammatical – rather than content – word classes: pronouns (*it*); adverbs (*there*); determiners (*that*).

An interesting way to begin a study of spoken language is to look at the words that occur most often, compared with the vocabulary of written language. In fact, the four most commonly used words sum up the interactive nature of speech:

The I and you.

The following research findings are taken from the CANCODE project (Cambridge and Nottingham University), based on a corpus of five million words of spoken language, alongside a similar corpus of written language (Carter 2004). The following lists show the most frequently used words in contemporary speech and writing.

Glossary
non-fluency features   interaction   vague language

The top 40 words

TABLE 14.1 The top forty words

Spoken language		Written language	
1	the	1	the
2	I	2	to
3	and	3	and
4	you	4	of
5	it	5	a
6	to	6	in
7	a	7	was

TABLE 14.1 Continued

Spoken language		Written language	
8	yeah	8	it
9	that	9	I
10	of	10	he
11	in	11	that
12	was	12	she
13	it's	13	for
14	know	14	on
15	mm	15	her
16	is	16	you
17	er	17	is
18	but	18	with
19	so	19	his
20	they	20	had
21	on	21	as
22	oh	22	at
23	we	23	but
24	have	24	be
25	no	25	have
26	laughs	26	from
27	well	27	not
28	like	28	they
29	what	29	by
30	do	30	this
31	right	31	are
32	just	32	were

TABLE 14.1 Continued

Spoken language		Written language	
33	he	33	all
34	for	34	him
35	erm	35	up
36	be	36	an
37	this	37	said
38	all	38	there
39	there	39	one
40	got	40	been

This statistical evidence highlights some interesting differences between the vocabulary used in spoken, as opposed to written, language. In writing, the most frequently used words are grammatical classes: determiners, pronouns, conjunctions, prepositions and auxiliary verbs. There are only a few content word classes, such as the main verb, 'said'. For obvious reasons, the voiced 'fillers' – *mm, er, erm* – are not common in written language. These **non-fluency features** can be explained by the spontaneous, unplanned nature of spoken language. But there are a number of other words that we use very often when speaking, but less frequently in writing.

Can such words be dismissed as simply informal or vague? Carter (ibid.) suggests that the essential quality of spoken language is that it is interactive, used to keep a dialogue between speakers open. Written language, on the other hand, is essentially a monologue, with little real possibility for **interaction** between writer and reader.

Go to www.routledge.com/cw/ross for Activity 14.1, Which asks pupils to reflect on the ways some common words function in spoken language.

Interaction

The interactive nature of speech is the significant factor in accounting for these differences between the vocabulary of spoken and written language. In written language, the writer must supply all the necessary information, as there is no chance for clarification. The use of **vague language** is a common feature of speech. This negative term suggests that these features are accidental and should be avoided if possible.

Carter (ibid.) prefers the term 'deliberately vague' language to indicate the ways that speakers interact. He suggests that precision is inappropriate in many informal contexts, that some hesitancy keeps the dialogue open. Pupils should be able to adapt their speaking style: what is appropriate between friends in casual conversation may not be effective in more public contexts. But there are some changes in attitudes towards levels of formality in speech.

Even in more formal situations these days the speaker may use tentative phrases, such as 'sort of' or 'kind of'. One effect is to make the speaker sound more 'human' and approachable. Tony Blair has been compared to Margaret Thatcher for his less assertive style of speaking in many contexts. This choice of style is clearly deliberate – he did not use it over the Iraq war, when a tone of authority was needed. I have also noticed, for example, that some recorded telephone promotional messages use a lot of 'ers' and 'ums' as a way of sounding more friendly, even though they have been deliberately scripted to sell something.

 Go to www.routledge.com/cw/ross for Activity 14.2, Identifying and commenting on the use of 'vague' language in spoken texts. **Y10+**

The word 'like' is very common in spoken language today (Number 28 in the CANCODE Top 40). But is it a single word or many in the same disguise? It is used in at least six different ways. Dictionaries list it as a verb, adjective, preposition, adverb, conjunction and noun. But the uses that are noted as 'informal', 'colloquial', 'slang', are more interesting for the study of spoken language.

'Like' can be used as an adverb 'It was a fair result, like', to add a note of caution. This use can follow nouns, verbs or adjectives, 'it was awesome like', but tends to come before them 'the band were like real.'

Recently a new use of 'like' has emerged: as a quotative to introduce direct speech: 'So I was like, you're so totally not going to wear that today, and she was like, Oh yes I am.' This functions like the standard 'I said … she said' and the colloquial 'I goes … she goes'.

Some researchers suggest that this use originates from west-coast USA and is used by the under 30s, possibly by more females than males. But this is open to investigation.

 Go to www.routledge.com/cw/ross for Activity 14.3, Looking at the use of 'like' in a transcript of teenage girls talking. **Y10+**

Grammar of spoken language

Glossary

ellipsis   compound sentences

Another striking feature of spoken language is the use of **ellipsis**. This term refers to abbreviated structures, often omitting the subject, such as:

Didn't know that film was on tonight.	*(I)*
Sounds good to me.	*(It, That)*
Lots of things to tell you about the trip to Barcelona.	*(There are)*

This is appropriate in spoken interaction but should only be used in written language to convey an informal, colloquial voice.

Research into spoken data shows that **compound sentence** structures are common: connecting clauses with the conjunctions 'and', 'but', 'or'.

 Go to www.routledge.com/cw/ross for Activity 14.4, Identifying examples of compound sentence structures in a transcript of spoken language. **Y10+**

The final chapter looks at new electronic forms of language. This channel of communication is sometimes called 'multi-modal' as it has introduced a fascinating cross-over of written and spoken styles of communication.

Electronic modes of language

The previous chapter outlined different channels of communication: Braille, sign language, writing and speaking. It looked at the ways some important differences between the physical situation of writing and speaking influence the language use, in particular the interactive nature of speaking. Although there are exceptions (a speech that has been carefully scripted; written notes that have been hastily scribbled) the situation for much writing and speaking differs in these ways:

Writing	Speaking
solitary	co-present
monologue	dialogue
time to plan	immediate
permanent	no record

But new electronic media lies somewhere between these extremes.

Go to www.routledge.com/cw/ross for Activity 15.1, Placing different types of electronic language on a spectrum between written and spoken language. **Y10+**

Interactive features of electronic language use

Glossary
personal pronouns   **interrogative**   **imperative**   **deixis**   **ellipsis**

The use of direct address – personal pronouns ('I' and 'you'), interrogatives and imperatives – is a feature of interactive language. Although spoken language is the most obviously interactive mode, some forms of written language are becoming more informal and conversational. Text books, for example, tend to address the reader directly with questions and instructions.

Look at the checklist at the end of the chapter.

How many of these terms do you understand?

Journalism articles often use a personal 'voice', as if the writer is speaking to an individual reader.

> *Lying in starts with the decision that your bed is the closest thing to earthly paradise and that you're going to stay in it. If it's a Saturday morning, a school holiday or the day after your tutorial, you can just turn over, make a little purring sound in the back of your throat and slip back into a warm fug.*

> ('How to Lie In', Guy Browning, The Guardian, *22 September, 2001*)

These types of written language only give the impression of interaction, however. The readers are not really personally known and do not have the opportunity to take their turn and reply. These are features that many electronic forms share with spoken language, creating a new cross-over style of communication.

 Go to www.routledge.com/cw/ross for Activity 15.2, Analysing interactive features in text-messages. **Y10+**

Spoken language can usually rely on a shared context, so it is not necessary to spell out all the details as precisely as in a written text. Ellipsis – omitting parts of the sentence structure – and deixis – using pronouns and adverbs to refer to shared knowledge – are common:

(I have) Been away.

I'll sort it (the dripping tap) tomorrow (Friday 3rd August).

At one time, mobile phone users tried to be as brief as possible to save money. There is no longer such a financial constraint; but people still want to save time. There is a shared acceptance that standards of conventional spelling, punctuation and style do not apply as strictly as in other written forms.

 Go to www.routledge.com/cw/ross for Activity 15.3, Identifying the use of ellipsis and deixis in text messages. **Y10+**

It is important to consider, not just the electronic mode, but all the other contextual factors that might influence language use:

- the participants and their relationship
- their purposes
- the topic

Participants: age, gender, occupation

There has been a myth in the media that it is young people who use non-standard language in their text messages and emails. But if you take an informal survey you may find that this is not the case any more. As older users of technology have started to use abbreviations and emoticons, so younger users have reverted to more standard written language.

 Go to www.routledge.com/cw/ross for Activity 15.4, Matching style of language use to identity of participants. **Y12+**

Use of writing to convey sound effects

Spoken language has various effects that are not present in a visual medium: volume, intonation, stress and emphasis. Writers have attempted to convey these in visual ways, such as:

- exclamation and question marks to show intonation;
- capital letters, bold font or underlining for volume and emphasis.

In the new electronic modes, users are developing innovative ways to capture the spirit of a live spoken interaction. Non-standard spelling can suggest the way a word is pronounced ('sooorry') Emoticons are used to represent facial expressions or mood.

 Go to www.routledge.com/cw/ross for Activity 15.5, Looking at examples from a social networking site. **Y12+**

There have already been so many variations in language use since people started using electronic modes to communicate. It is likely that styles will continue to develop until there is a dominant style accepted by most users. Unlike most written genres, it may be younger people who set the conventions and older users who follow their lead.

References

Abley, M. (2003) *Spoken Here: Travel among Threatened Languages*. London: Arrow.

Aitchison, J. (1996) *The Seeds of Speech*. Cambridge: Cambridge University Press.

Bierce, A. (2003) *The Devil's Dictionary*. London: Bloomsbury.

Blake, J., Shortis, T., Powell, A. with Osborn, P. and Bailey, A. (2011) *All Talk English 14–19*. BT (www.bt.com/alltalk).

Brown, J. (1971) *Programmed Vocabulary*. Englewood Cliffs, NJ: Prentice-Hall.

Chomsky, N. (1970) *Language and Freedom*. New York: Harcourt Brace Jovanovich.

Crystal, D. (1995) *The Cambridge Encyclopedia of the English Language*. Cambridge: Cambridge University Press.

Crystal, D. (1998) *Language Play*. Harmondsworth: Penguin.

Crystal, D. (2001) *Language and the Internet*. Cambridge: Cambridge University Press.

DfEE/QCA (2000) *The National Curriculum: Handbook for Secondary Teachers in England: Key Stages 3 and 4*. London: HMSO.

DfES (2001) *The Framework for Teaching English: Years 7, 8 and 9*. London: HMSO.

English and media centre (2010) *Investigating Spoken language*. London: EMC.

Fairclough, N. (2000) *New Labour, New Language*. London: Routledge.

Firth, J.R. (1964) *Tongues of Men and Speech*. Oxford: Oxford University Press.

Fowler, H. (1965) *Dictionary of Modern English Usage* (2nd edn). Oxford: Oxford University Press.

Freire, P. (1970) *Pedagogy of the Oppressed*. New York: Herder and Herder.

Freire, P. (1973) *Education for Critical Consciousness*. New York: Herder and Herder.

Goddard, A. (1996) 'Tall Stories: the metaphorical nature of everyday talk'. *English Education*, 30(2). NATE (The National Association for the Teaching of English).

Hathorn, L. and Rogers, G. (1994) *Way Home*. London: Andersen Press.

Hodges, R. (1982) *Improving Spelling and Vocabulary in the Secondary School*. ERIC Clearinghouse on Reading, and Communication Skills.

Holmes, J. (1992) *An Introduction to Sociolinguistics*. London: Longman.

Hudson, R. (1980) *Sociolinguistics*. Cambridge: Cambridge University Press.

Köhler, W. (1947) *Gestalt Psychology*. New York: Liveright.

McWhorter, J. (1998) *The Word on the Street*, New York: Perseus Books.

Peccei, J. (1994) *Child Language*. London: Routledge.

Perfors, A. (2004) *What's in a Name? The effect of sound symbolism on perception of facial attractiveness*. Poster presented at CogSci, Chicago.

Pinker, S. (1994) *The Language Instinct*. London: Harper Collins.

Raleigh, W. (1926) *On Writers and Writing* (selected and edited by George Gordon). London: Kessinger.

Rosen, M. (2003) emagazine, 15. English and media centre.

Sapir, E. (1970) *Language: An Introduction to the Study of Speech*. London: Hart-Davies.

Tomlinson, D. (1994) 'Errors in the research into the effectiveness of grammar teaching.' *English in Education*, 28: 2–26.

Wales, K. (2004) *A Dictionary of Stylistics*. Harlow: Longman.

Weekley, E. (1929) *The English Language*. London: André Deutsch.

Wilkinson, A. (1971) *The Foundations of Language: Talking and Reading in Young Children*. Oxford: Oxford University Press.

Index